ACTIVE
English

Learning Strategies That Will Have
Your Students Asking,
Is That the Bell *Already?*

Karla Hardaway

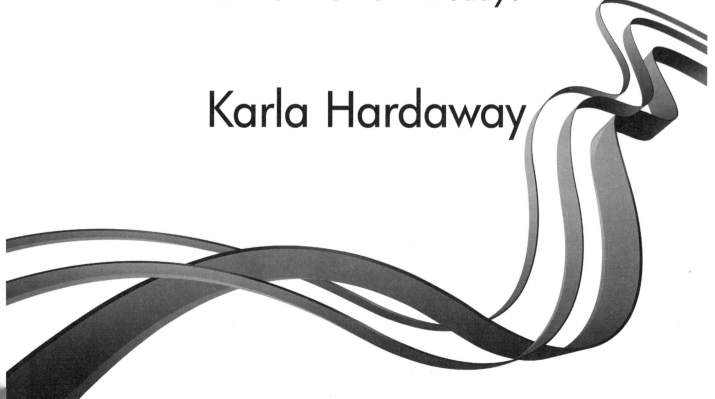

Requests for permission, other than personal classroom use, should be addressed to:

Cottonwood Press
109-B Cameron Drive
Fort Collins, Colorado 80525
1-800-864-4297
www.cottonwoodpress.com

ISBN 978-1-877673-96-2
Printed in the United States of America

To teachers who dream of changing the world
by reaching one student at a time.

TABLE OF CONTENTS

TABLE OF CONTENTS

ON THEIR FEET—ACTIVITIES FOR SPEECH, DRAMA, AND SPECIAL OCCASIONS

LISTS, LISTS, LISTS—FOR FREEWRITES, SKITS, COMPOSITION, IMPROVISATION, SPEECH, AND PLAYING WITH LANGUAGE

APPENDIX

INTRODUCTION

»MY CREATIVE WRITING STUDENTS call themselves "chicken slaves." Each class begins with freewrites. Pens move across paper for ten minutes until my chicken-shaped kitchen timer dings. Then there's a flurry of hands as students volunteer to read what they've written.

My sophomore English students don't do as many freewrites (in spite of constant begging), but we fill their ninety minute class with other writing activities, skits, and drama games that they enjoy. At the end of class, I get the nicest compliments:

- Is that the bell already?
- Time passes by so fast in here.
- Do I have to go to my next class?
- I want to stay in here all day.

So what is my success secret? I use active learning strategies in my classroom, involving students directly and actively in their own learning. Students learn so much better when they read, write, speak, listen, reflect, act, and play games instead of being passive "receivers of knowledge." Learning becomes a social event; students learn almost without realizing it because they are having fun.

I have been teaching English for thirty-four years. During that time I have taught every grade level from seven through twelve and every ability level—basic, general, honors, and gifted. Among other things, I have taught English, creative writing, speech, debate, drama, and film as literature. I have found that active learning strategies benefit *all* kinds of students. Each student participates at his or her own level and is encouraged to improve through interaction with others.

USING THIS BOOK. *Active English* is a book that English, speech, and drama teachers can easily use to augment their textbook and to find ideas quickly and easily. The activities concentrate on improving reading comprehension and writing skills and also help improve public speaking skills. The activities are appropriate for English and speech classes, grades 8-12, with

INTRODUCTION

the materials complementing curriculum already in place in many districts. The activities require few materials that aren't already available in most classrooms.

The book is divided into five main sections:

- **WRITING PROSE.** A wide variety of writing activities that have proven very successful in many classrooms.

- **LITERATURE.** Activities that help students understand and write fiction.

- **WRITING POETRY.** Active learning prompts that help unleash creativity.

- **ON THEIR FEET.** Activities for speech, drama, and special occasions.

- **LISTS, LISTS, LISTS.** Practical lists to use for freewrites, skits, composition, improvisation, speech, and playing with language.

A FEW NOTES ABOUT WRITING. Sometimes teachers avoid teaching writing because they feel inadequate as writers themselves or because they don't know how to teach writing. Many can dissect classic literature but don't know how to teach a child to write a poem. If teachers try the writing activities in this book along with their students, they may gain confidence in their own writing ability.

Teachers may also avoid teaching writing because they don't have time to prepare writing lessons or dread the time required for grading. However, not all writing activities require traditional grading, and the benefits of writing are too great to be ignored.

For example, when students write about what they are reading, they are forced to process the information more fully. Writing helps students think, organize, and reflect on what they have read. Students become more engaged with the material; they retain more of the content. When students use written material as a pattern to create their own material, they are operating at the top levels of higher order thinking skills. They are analyzing the material, determining the implications made, figuring out the writer's reasoning, and then formulating their own writing.

After students write poetry themselves, they are better able to get inside the heads of poets and understand their poems. When students write stories, their imaginations are awakened; they appreciate the writing process that the short story or novel writer has gone through. When students write about what they are reading, they are forced to interact with the text.

ABOUT USING DRAMA. Teachers who avoid using drama in the classroom are missing out on one of the most valuable tools available for learning. Drama develops creativity and self-confidence. Students engage in the process of self-discovery. They develop critical thinking and organizational skills. They have fun and experience a healthy release of emotion. They learn respect and admiration for others and develop group socialization skills. They are forced to listen and to read the body language of others. Because they are having fun, they remember what they learn.

As students improve communication skills, they become more self-confident. Taking risks in class in front of an audience teaches students to trust their ideas and abilities. This trust spills over into success in school, careers, and life. As students become more articulate and organized, they begin to communicate more effectively with others orally and in writing. Students learn empathy for others, cooperation skills, problem solving skills, self-discipline, memory focus, aesthetic appreciation, and so much more.

As a final note, for anyone who doubts the importance of active learning, here are some quotations to ponder:

Learning is not a spectator sport. (D. Blocher)

Tell me and I'll forget; show me and I may remember; involve me and I'll understand.
(Chinese proverb)

We learn more by looking for the answer to a question and not finding it than we do
from learning the answer itself. (Lloyd Alexander, American author)

It is the supreme art of the teacher to awaken joy in creative expression
and knowledge. (Albert Einstein)

You don't understand anything until you learn it
more than one way. (Marvin Minsky)

The biggest enemy to learning is the talking teacher. (John Holt)

Karla Hardaway

WRITING
PROSE

A Variety of High-Interest Activities

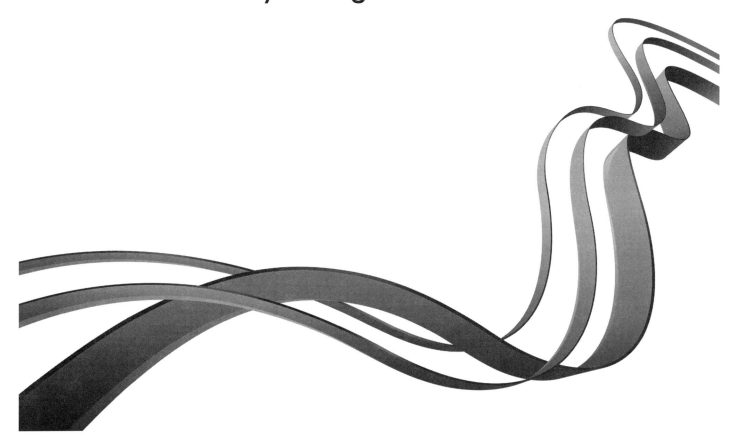

ALL ABOUT ME

»COMPLETE THE FOLLOWING SENTENCES quickly with whatever thoughts enter your mind. When everyone finishes, we will share some of our answers. This activity will help you get to know your class members and your teacher.

1. If I could, I would...

2. I like to read...

3. The most urgent problem facing the world today is...

4. Happiness is...

5. If I were a teacher...

6. My parents...

7. I wish...

8. Given a million dollars, I would...

9. Too many people...

10. Boredom is...

11. My favorite activity is...

12. The role of people in this world is...

13. If I weren't in school today, I would be...

14. Sadness is...

15. The worst day of my life was...

16. I like the color _____ because...

17. The most important event in my life so far has been...

18. I hope that...

19. The most perfect age is_____ because...

20. My strongest asset is...

21. Within five years I would like to...

22. My worst fault is...

23. School is...

24. I hate to read...

25. Humanity's greatest accomplishment has been...

CLASS WRITE-A-THON

»HAVE STUDENTS ARRANGE THEIR DESKS IN A CIRCLE. Give them a topic to write about and set the timer for ten minutes. (Try the "Lists" section of this book, pages 107-131, for topic ideas.)

Students should write for the entire ten minutes. They may write a story, a poem, a personal opinion, a rant, or whatever they like, but the idea is to write freely. They do not need to be concerned with spelling, grammar, punctuation, etc., although it is quite acceptable if they write correctly. They do not need to take time to self-edit as they write.

At the end of ten minutes, go around the circle and have students read their freewrites aloud. If someone writes something very personal, the student may skip reading aloud once during the activity, but only once. After someone reads, the members of the class are not allowed to make comments, clap, or ask questions. That includes the teacher. The lack of feedback frees the writers from worry about reactions of the class.

When everyone has had a chance to read, choose another topic and have students write again for ten minutes. Repeat the reading aloud process. Do this as many times as possible in a class period. The students will begin to loosen up and find their voices.

By the time you finish this activity, you will have established a writing environment in your classroom. My students always comment on how much fun they have doing this and beg me to let them have a write-a-thon again. I am amazed that I am able to get them to write for ninety minutes (we're on block schedule) and they think it's fun.

You don't need to collect the freewrites to grade. Just give each student points for participation.

PUNCTUATING TOM SWIFTIES

»TOM SWIFTIES ARE PUNS formed by using overly descriptive adverbs and verbs in writing conversation. The name "Tom Swifty" comes from a character named Tom Swift in a series of books published since 1910 under the pseudonym Victor Appleton. The exaggerated use of descriptive adverbs and verbs in these books is often comical, even to the point of creating puns.

As you read and enjoy the following Tom Swifties, try to figure out the puns.

1. "I'm lost for words," said Tom speechlessly.
2. "Oh, I've dropped the toothpaste," said Tom, crestfallen.
3. "I am not a dummy," Tom said lifelessly.
4. "S-s-s-s-stop!" Tom said haltingly.
5. "I won't let a flat tire get me down," Tom despaired.
6. "I keep banging my head on things," Tom said bashfully.
7. "I haven't caught a fish all day!" Tom said without debate.
8. "She said I look like a common farm animal," Tom said sheepishly.
9. "I hope you like the gift I bought," Tom said presently.
10. "I've been on a diet," Tom expounded.

For review in punctuating dialogue, see if you can punctuate the following Tom Swifties correctly.

1. Isn't that baby bird cute Tom chirped.

2. I'm a mime Tom said wordlessly.

3. But I wanted a purebred dog Tom howled.

4. I'm losing my hair Tom bawled.

5. I can't believe I ate the whole pineapple Tom said dolefully.

6. That's the last time I'll ever pet a lion Tom said offhandedly.

7. The kids have eaten all the potato chips Tom said crisply.

8. I can't find my seat belt Tom said without restraint.

9. I'll never sleep on the railroad tracks again Tom said, beside himself.

10. I'm not swimming in the deep end Tom said shallowly.

GROUP TOM SWIFTIES

»MODERN WRITERS GENERALLY USE PLAIN DIALOGUE TAGS ("he said" and "she said," for example). Tom Swifties use exaggerated dialogue tags, which are discouraged in serious writing. However, Tom Swifties do show that dialogue tags can interrupt the flow of speech and sometimes be ridiculous. That's why it's fun—and instructive—to have students give them a try. Writing them also gives students practice in punctuating quotations correctly.

Divide students into groups of four. Each group must write ten new Tom Swifties that have not been read in class. The students must punctuate the lines of dialogue correctly. When all the groups are finished, have each group read its new Tom Swifties to the class. Supplying each group with a list of adverbs may help students in constructing the new Tom Swifties. Here is one list:

SAMPLE LIST OF ADVERBS FOR TOM SWIFTIES

absentmindedly	famously	inhumanely	noisily	sheepishly
accidentally	freely	inhumanly	oafishly	sloppily
acidly	fully	inwardly	openly	smoothly
afterwards	girlishly	jazzily	owlishly	speedily
annually	greatly	jokingly	painfully	surprisingly
bashfully	gushingly	lengthily	parenthetically	sweetly
bleakly	heavily	lifelessly	passively	thankfully
blindly	highly	lightly	patiently	tightly
briefly	hourly	limply	playfully	unevenly
brightly	icily	loosely	pokily	utterly
brutally	identically	manually	poorly	upwardly
cheerfully	illegibly	mechanically	probingly	vacantly
colorfully	illuminated	messily	profoundly	vaguely
crossly	imaginatively	moistly	promptly	warmly
daily	impassively	motherly	rarely	weakly
deeply	impatiently	moodily	recklessly	wholly
dimly	impishly	mushily	rigidly	willfully
doubtfully	inaudibly	mutely	sedately	wishfully
dreamily	incidentally	mysteriously	separately	yearly
equally	increasingly	nakedly	shakily	yieldingly
eventually	indefinitely	noiselessly	sharply	zestfully

TABLOID STORY

»ASK STUDENTS TO OBTAIN COPIES OF TABLOID NEWSPAPERS. The activity is more fun if the papers are different, so you might want to give them several weeks to find a copy. Also, several students (two or three) may share a paper.

On a designated day, ask students to bring their papers to read in class. They will have fun laughing at the ridiculous articles. Then have each person select an article to change into a short story. The newspaper article merely gives the details. The short story will tell the reasons for the event. The plot should include the basic situation (exposition), rising action, climax, falling action, and resolution. It should also include dialogue. Students should make up the parts that are not in the article.

Some of my favorite student stories were about an armadillo who was in love with a lawnmower, a man who was obsessed with having a limb amputated, a girl who lost her leg to a shark on her honeymoon, and a wedding performed in a hot air balloon.

Regular newspaper articles will also work, but they may not be so bizarre.

For an example of a student tabloid story written using the newspaper headline "Patient Begs Doctor to Cut off His Leg," see Appendix, page 135.

SHOW AND TELL

»YOUNG CHILDREN LOVE TO BRING ITEMS to school for "show and tell." But I have discovered that high school students also love show and tell.

I ask students to bring something to class that has meaning for them. They will show the object to the class and explain its story.

Students place their desks in a circle. We go around the circle and each person shows his/her object and tells its story. Everyone else takes notes on the person and the object. At the end of the activity, everyone has taken notes on all the objects. Each person must then write a story that includes at least eight of the objects.

The most unusual object ever brought was "Ed, the Head." This was a clear glass jar in the shape and size of a human head. Many students bring jewelry, stuffed animals, pictures, statues, trophies, dolls, etc.

For one show and tell, my object was a beautiful jeweled bracelet given to me when I was eighteen by the first boy who ever said he loved me. After I received the bracelet, I stopped dating the boy because I realized that he cared more about me than I did about him. But I did keep the bracelet. Years later, I realized that the stones (rubies and sapphires) were real. After that particular show and tell, many students included Mrs. Hardaway, the heartbreaker, in their stories.

Whatever form they take, the stories are always a lot of fun.

ELEVATOR STORY

»IT'S EASY TO WRITE A SUSPENSE STORY using an elevator story model. Here's the procedure:

1. Take a large group of characters who are strangers and cram them into an elevator.

2. Use a mix of people who are experiencing personal problems, including someone with a psychological problem or anger issue. Include various genders and ages.

3. Now make the elevator stop between floors.

4. If more complications are needed, have the vent fan stop working.

5. Add a time deadline by having a medical emergency.

This model creates a rather artificial scenario, but it works. The basic situation involves people in an elevator. The rising action begins when the elevator stops. The conflict is driven by a person with a psychological problem or anger issue. The climax occurs when that person loses control. The falling action begins when the characters know help is on the way. The resolution is when the elevator doors open, or perhaps when the elevator falls to destruction.

Now, here's the twist. The elevator doesn't need to be a real elevator. Just think of a way to bring a group of diverse people together and trap them in a dangerous situation. The elevator might be a sinking ship (*Titanic*), a crashed airplane (*Lost*), a hostage situation (*Speed*), an erupting volcano (*Volcano*), a bomb scare (*88 Minutes*), a hospital under quarantine (*Pandemic*), etc.

Now write your elevator story.

MEMOIRS

»MEMOIRS ARE ONE OF THE MOST POPULAR FORMS of writing today. Although memoirs are based on a person's real-life experiences, they read more like fiction.

A memoir usually focuses on one event or time of life that has great meaning to an author. It not only tells what happened, but it also records the person's reaction to what happened. Some events stay with us all our lives, almost as if they are burned into our memories and rehearsed in our dreams. The events may seem inconsequential to others, but for some reason they affect us personally in a profound way.

Are memoirs always true? The answer is, "Yes and no." One person may remember an event differently from another person. For example, two brothers telling about growing up with an alcoholic parent may tell very different versions of events that happened. What each remembers is his reality clouded by his own experiences and emotions.

How is a memoir different from an autobiography? Autobiographies are typically written in chronological order and are grounded in verifiable facts. They cover an entire life. Memoirs, on the other hand, often focus on a particular time or a particular event. They often go into more depth about the person's reactions to particular life struggles, defeats, and successes. The memories are also less likely to be told in chronological order.

WRITE

Write a memoir of your own. First brainstorm and write a list of at least five significant events in your life. Possible events might be a family move, the death of a loved one, your first love, an accomplishment, a family vacation, a school event, etc. The event must be important to you, regardless of how others perceive it. You may go back as far as you can remember. Family stories make good memoirs. Or you may go back to yesterday or last week.

Your teacher will divide the class into groups of four. Share your list with the others in your group, explaining why each event is significant to you. Group members may help clarify events by asking questions or asking for more details. Groups should help each member choose one event that will make the best story.

After meeting with your group, begin to write your story. Don't try to tell everything that happened before the event. Just begin. Include conversations, details about setting, facial expressions, etc., to put the reader "there" with you. Try to show us how you felt by describing your actions, rather than simply telling us what you felt. Let us experience the event with you and draw the same conclusions you did.

GRAVEYARD SCAVENGER HUNT

»YOUR CLASS WILL BE VISITING AN OLD GRAVEYARD. You will be taking notes and taking photos of tombstones for a class project—a scavenger hunt. Your job is to come prepared and to be observant as you try to complete all the items below.

Be sure to carry a notebook to record your answers. You should copy relevant information (names, birth and death dates, epitaphs, etc.) from each tombstone to prove each answer. You may also want to take pictures or make a sketch of unusual ones.

1. What is the layout of the graveyard? (Are the areas divided in any way—old vs. new, afflu-ent vs. poor? Are any sections segregated by ethnicity, race, or religion? Is the graveyard full, or are there still areas for new graves?)

2. As you walk around, write down six epitaphs that you find interesting.

3. Try to find graves for a veteran from each of the following wars: Civil War, Spanish American War, World War I, World War II, Korean War, Vietnam War, and other con-flicts (Be sure to tell which one). Also see if you can find a veteran of two or more wars.

4. Find the family plot of what seems to be an affluent family. List all names, dates and rela-tionships for members. Explain why you think this family was affluent.

5. Find the grave of what seems to be a poor person. Explain why you think this person was poor.

6. Find a child's grave (someone who died before age 10). Is there anything to suggest the child died in an epidemic or an accident? If so, what?

7. Find an unusual marker. Is it unusual because of artistry (picture, sculpture, design, etc.) or modern additions (photographs, symbols, etc.)? Explain.

8. Look for the oldest grave and the newest grave.

When you return to class, choose one of the following writing activities to complete:

1. Write a fictional short story or poem inspired by one of the epitaphs you recorded.

2. Research one of the people from the graves you viewed. Find out as much as you can about the individual and write a report you might share with a descendent of that person.

WE'RE ALL THE SAME CHARACTER

»THIS ACTIVITY HELPS A CLASS LEARN to create three-dimensional characters for writing stories or acting. It can also help them brainstorm story ideas.

Seat the class in a circle. Begin by stating the age, gender, or occupation of a character. (After students are familiar with the activity, a student may begin.) The entire class then "becomes" this character, each person speaking as the character and adding significant details about the character or past events in the character's life.

The first few people add details about significant relationships, attitudes, and experiences. When one person finishes, he or she points to another person in the circle and that person continues. Everyone in the circle must contribute something, and it must fit into the whole.

After the activity, ask students to describe in writing how they would feel about the person the group created if they came in contact with the character in real life. Another possible follow-up activity is to have students write a new chapter in the collective character's life.

Here's an example of how the conversation might proceed:

Teacher: My name is Sally White. I have just enrolled in your school as a sophomore. I have just walked into your English class.

Student #1: Gosh I hate being new. Why is everyone staring at me? I wish I were invisible. I really wish I were back at my old school in New York. Why did my dad have to get transferred? I wonder if they can tell how scared I am.

Student #2: The teacher seems nice. Kind of an airhead, but nice. I think I'll sit next to this cute boy. He kind of reminds me of my boyfriend I left behind.

Student #3: That was the hardest part. Telling Brandon that I had to move back to Louisiana with my parents. He cried like a baby. We really love each other. Someday we were going to get...That boy is really cute! He's smiling at me!

Student #4: Brandon always said I was a total flirt...The move should be better in some ways. Mom and Dad were both working so much they never had much time for me.

Student #5: We are staying with my grandparents for now. It's okay, but it's like having four parents. My grandmother wants me to clean the kitchen all the time and come home at eight o'clock. Ha! My parents hardly ever even noticed what time I came home before. That was one nice thing about parents who work all the time.

As they add details, the students will actually begin to create the beginnings of a story centered around the character's life. Each student's imagination may be triggered by what another student adds. The story should evolve. (Don't be afraid to intervene if it goes too far off track.)

MOVIE REVIEW

»FIRST WATCH THE MOVIE you would like to review. Then complete the following items, using complete sentences:

1. WRITE A SHORT SUMMARY OF THE MOVIE, possibly three or four sentences long. A summary of the movie *Twilight* might read as follows: "*Twilight* is an entertaining movie that appeals mostly to teenagers and young adults. It takes place in a high school in Washington State. The actors are young and quick to fall in love, in spite of many complications. The main character Bella is a human and her love interest is a vampire."

2. IS THE PLOT BELIEVABLE? IS THE DIALOGUE NATURAL? Be sure to include both strengths and weaknesses, referring to specific examples or scenes in the movie. For example, a discussion of *Twilight's* plot might include the following: "The plot is simple enough, but the intensity of the love between Bella and Edward seems forced and unbelievable. She spends most of her time staring at him, showing her front teeth while he shares secrets of the vampire world. She visits the vampires' home but doesn't fear for her life or seem to care that she is in grave danger because everyone there wants to drink her blood. As for Edward, he is hundreds of years old, yet he has never been in love before. That is hard to believe. Also unbelievable is the fact that Edward is able to miss many days of school (all sunny days), but he never suffers any consequences from his absences."

3. WERE THE ACTORS WELL CHOSEN FOR THE FILM? Be specific as you discuss the casting. An example of a review of *Twilight*: "The actress chosen to play Bella Swan looks the part. However, she comes off at times as too unemotional. The actor who plays Edward is very handsome and fits the part. He is probably the force that keeps the movie going. The actress who plays Rosalie seems too old, and she has dark roots in her blonde hair. Do vampires really bleach their hair? Carlisle is believable enough, but his make-up is way too white and caked on. The actress who plays Alice really fits the part. Her haircut is perky and fun like her personality. She actually could pass for a teenager. The scene where Edward shows his skin in the sunlight is well done. He glistens without overdoing it."

4. MEET WITH OTHER CLASS MEMBERS IN A SMALL GROUP TO SHARE REVIEWS. As you listen to other reviews, jot down points of agreement and disagreement for discussion. Be prepared to respond to those who react to what you have said, as well.

IMAGERY: WE'RE GOING TO FLY!

»IMAGERY IS LANGUAGE that creates mental images or emotions that appeal to the five senses—especially sight, but also hearing, taste, touch, and smell. It uses figurative language such as simile and metaphor.

EXERCISE

Ask students to stand beside their desks and close their eyes. Tell them they're going to go on an imaginary journey. They are to concentrate on your voice. Tell them to imagine the following:

1. First walk out on a balcony. Feel the warm air on your skin. Smell the flowers in the pot sitting on the corner of the balcony. You hear a car horn honking so you look over the edge of the railing. An orange Volkswagen is passing by.

2. You see two squirrels playing in the street. They don't see the approaching car. You let out a scream without thinking just as they scurry to safety.

3. Now you notice a bird eating some trash on the side of the street. It flies away. In fact, it flies so close to you in the balcony that you reach out to touch it. As you reach, you fall over the railing.

4. You feel yourself falling. But then you begin to flap your arms and fly! It's a feeling of freedom you have never before experienced! You feel the air rushing by. You look down below. The people and cars are so small.

5. Now you land in a tree. You enjoy the noises around you. But you begin to think about your homework and you miss your mom.

6. You take off from the tree and fly back to your balcony. You land lightly. You wave good-bye to the outside and turn to the door.

7. You're inside. You hear the door latch as it closes.

WRITING ACTIVITY

1. Now have students sit down immediately and write about the experience, describing in detail what they saw, heard, smelled, and touched.

2. Then allow students to read their reactions aloud. Remind students to note imagery in what their classmates read.

"HEAVY ARM" FOLLOW-UP

After "We're Going to Fly," students will have had some experience with imagery. Then try the "Heavy Arm" exercise.

1. Ask students to stand beside their desks and hold the arm they do not write with out to the side perpendicular to their body. They should not put their arms down until you give permission. When holding it out has become very difficult, let them put their arms down.

2. Tell the students to sit down and quickly write what their arms felt like at the beginning, middle, and end of the exercise.

3. Ask students to read their papers aloud.

LITERATURE

Activities that Help Students
Understand Fiction

GRAFFITI EXCHANGE

»THIS ACTIVITY MAY BE USED AS AN INTRODUCTION TO A TOPIC or as a culminating activity. Write an open-ended question on the board. Ask half of the students to go to the board and write a response to the question, writing high enough on the board to leave room for a second response. When finished, they should sign their names and take their seats.

Then ask the rest of the students to go to the board and write a response to one of the responses already on the board. They may agree or disagree with the original response as long as they justify their answers.

When all students are seated, ask each student to read aloud what he or she wrote. You may need to ask the students additional questions to clarify their responses. The sharing will generate discussion and lead to a lively interaction of ideas.

Here are some possible questions.

1. Is telling the truth always important?

2. Should love require sacrifice?

3. Which is more important, intelligence or appearance?

4. Why do people write?

5. What makes something a work of art?

6. What do you expect the future to be like?

7. Is experience the best teacher?

8. How important is your own personal privacy?

9. What qualities make a person a hero?

10. Are old ways the best ways?

11. Are wars always worthwhile?

12. Is the price of freedom ever too high?

(continued)

GRAFFITI EXCHANGE

Here are some prompts that are specific to works of literature:

1. Which is more important, the personal freedoms outlined in the Bill of Rights or personal safety? (Use to begin a discussion about guarding personal freedoms, the warning in George Orwell's novel *1984*.)

2. All men are created equal. Is this a true statement? Justify your answer. (Use to introduce Kurt Vonnegut's short story "Harrison Bergeron.")

3. Do you believe in love at first sight? Justify your answer. (Use to introduce William Shakespeare's play *Romeo and Juliet*.)

4. Could you ever justify disobeying the law? Explain. (Use to introduce Sophocles' play *Antigone*.)

5. What kinds of walls separate people? (Use to discuss Robert Frost's poem "Mending Wall.")

6. Is stealing wrong? (Use to introduce Victor Hugo's novel *Les Miserables*.)

7. Should valuable heirlooms be used? (Use to discuss Alice Walker's short story "Everyday Use.")

8. Which of your senses, sight or hearing, could you most easily live without? (Use to introduce Helen Keller's book *The Story of My Life*.)

9. What lessons do people learn by studying the Holocaust? (Use to discuss Anne Frank's book *The Diary of a Young Girl*.)

10. What makes a person popular? Is popularity important? (Use to discuss Katherine Mansfield's short story "The Doll's House.")

11. Is ambition always a good attribute? (Use to introduce Shakespeare's play *Julius Caesar*.)

12. Has technology made our lives better or worse? (Use to discuss Henry David Thoreau's book *Walden*.)

Students love to write on chalkboards or white boards. You may also use dry-erase markers and let them write on any slick surface such as walls or windows. You'll be surprised how quiet and involved students will be during this activity.

PLOT STRUCTURE GAME

»ASK STUDENTS TO EXPLAIN THE FOLLOWING quotation and then tell why they agree or disagree with it.

> "There are only two or three human stories,
> and they go on repeating themselves as fiercely
> as if they had never happened before."
> —Willa Cather

Introduce the idea that many scholars say there are very few basic story plots. Some of the plots include "overcoming the monster," "rags to riches," "the quest," and "the romance." Each plot can be summarized simply. For example, "the romance" might be summarized as "Boy meets girl; boy loses girl; boy gets girl back."

To give students practice reducing a plot to its bare essentials, ask them to write on a sheet of paper a three-sentence summary of a movie they have seen. The sentences should be as concise as possible, but they should cover the beginning, middle, and end of the movie. The idea is to reduce the story to the bare bones or skeleton of the plot. The sentences may be a bit vague, but not so vague that their classmates cannot guess the name of the movie.

Here are some examples:

- Girl nerd and boy jock fall in love.
- Friends trick the couple into breaking up.
- Girl and boy make up and sing in musical.
  (*High School Musical*)

- Young white teen runs away from abusive dad.
- Teen and friend hide in home of three African-American women.
- Oldest African-American woman adopts young teen.
  (*The Secret Life of Bees*)

- Boy tries to change nerdy girl.
- Boy and nerdy girl fall in love.
- Nerdy girl dies.
  (*A Walk to Remember*)

- Girl falls in love with boy from another world.
- Girl loses voice and almost loses boy.
- Girl kisses boy and gets boy and voice back.
  (*The Little Mermaid*)

(continued)

PLOT STRUCTURE GAME

Allow students to read their sentences aloud and ask members of the class to guess what movies they summarize. Students will discover that many sentence summaries could stand for more than one movie. The activity actually suggests the truth of Willa Cather's quote.

After doing the three-sentence summaries with your students, go on to teach basic plot elements—exposition, rising action, climax, denouement.

TANDEM STORIES

»TANDEM STORIES ARE WRITTEN IN PAIRS. Assign partners or let the students choose partners.

1. Review some basic parts of a traditional short story: exposition, rising action, climax, and denouement.

2. Instruct students to begin writing a story, starting with exposition. After about five minutes, have the partners exchange papers. Each student continues the other person's story. The story should flow so that an audience hearing the story would think that one person wrote it.

3. As the process continues, instruct students to exchange papers with their partners every five minutes or so. Remind students to include rising action, climax, and denouement, doing the best they can and understanding that the results are not going to be perfect, given the time limit. The process should take from twenty-five to forty-five minutes, total, depending on how many times the papers are exchanged.

4. When the stories are complete, have the students read aloud their stories to the class. (Or break the class into small groups, and have students read aloud to their group members.) Each pair will have written two short stories.

BOOK JOURNAL QUESTIONS

»EVERY DAY, AT THE END OF CLASS READING TIME, answer that day's journal questions below, based on the portion of the book you have just read. Keep all of your questions together until your teacher collects them.

Start by citing the title and author of the book. Before answering the questions each day, record the page on which you began reading and the page on which you ended reading. (You may read outside of class, as well, of course.) Each journal answer should be at least one-half to one page long.

Day 1. Before reading your book, describe the cover. What do you think the cover reveals about the story? What does the back or inside cover say about the book? The author? Why did you choose this book to read?

Day 2. What key elements are introduced in the exposition? Make three predictions of what will happen in the book based on the opening pages.

Day 3. Who seems to be the major character (or characters)? Is this person like you or anyone else you know? Explain.

Day 4. What role does the setting play in the book? Try setting the book in another place and describe what effect that would have on the story.

Day 5. Which characters are round characters and which characters are flat characters? Explain. Are there any characters that you can't classify yet?

Day 6. Does the author use foreshadowing or flashback? Give some examples of each if possible.

Day 7. Do your characters like each other? Explain your answer.

Day 8. What point of view does the author use to tell the story? How does the point of view affect the story?

Day 9. What is the major conflict of the novel? How do you think it will be resolved?

Day 10. Does the book teach any lessons? Explain.

Day 11. Summarize the book's ending. Were any of your predictions in question number two correct? Explain.

Day 12. Would you recommend this book to a friend? Why or why not?

POINT OF VIEW SKITS

»DEFINE DIFFERENT TYPES OF POINT OF VIEW for your students. Although there are many approaches to point of view, it makes sense to start with three commonly used types:

1. Omniscient—The "all-knowing" narrator. A godlike narrator tells the story. The narrator knows about all the characters—their past, present, and future. The narrator can take us into the minds of all the characters.

2. First person—A character in the story tells the story. The narrator uses first person pronouns (I, me, my, us, etc.) and can take us into his or her own mind only.

3. Limited third person—A narrator tells the story through the eyes of, usually, one character only. We know only what that one character is thinking.

Now ask two students to perform a skit for the class to watch. For example, you might give them this scenario:

A teenage girl walks into her brother's room as he is trying on her earring.
She wants her earring back. He wants to keep it.

(For other ideas, consult the "Lists" section of this book, pages 109-131.) When the skit is over, ask students to write what happened, but assign different points of view to each row. Example:

Rows 1 and 2 use omniscient point of view.

Row 3 uses first person point of view from the girl's point of view.

Row 4 uses first person point of view from the boy's point of view.

Row 5 uses limited third person through the girl.

Row 6 uses limited third person through the boy.

Ask several students to read their accounts aloud, being sure to get samples of each point of view. Ask class members to point out the differences in each point of view. The differences will become quite evident as students read.

CHARACTERIZATION

»THIS ACTIVITY WILL HELP STUDENTS to become familiar with characterization methods, particularly indirect methods. When authors make explicit statements about what a character is like, they are using direct characterization. When they reveal what a character is like through descriptions of the character's appearance, speech, actions, and interactions with others, they are using indirect characterization.

EXAMPLES

Direct characterization: *John is kind and generous.*

Indirect characterization: *When John realized that Mary had forgotten her lunch, he insisted on sharing his lunch with her.* (We conclude that John is kind and generous because he shares his lunch.)

LOOKING AT CHARACTERIZATION

1. Have students perform some of the following impromptu skits. Each skit requires three students. You may have students perform as many skits as you like, but two skits may be sufficient.

    Here are some skit ideas:

    *   Two students are talking about the beauty pageant held at the high school over the weekend. They are talking about the winner when she walks in.
    *   A girl is talking to another girl about her blind date over the weekend. Then the boy walks in.
    *   Two teachers are talking about a student who causes trouble. Then the student walks up.
    *   Two people are discussing their friend who has bad breath. Then the friend walks up.

2. The class watches the skits and then chooses one of the skits to analyze. Write the skit characters' names across the board, and then lead the class in brainstorming a list of adjectives or phrases to describe each character.

3. As you make each list, ask the students to tell you how they know this person is disloyal, cocky, angry, etc. They will cite things the characters said, voice inflections, facial expressions, body language, etc.

(continued)

» continued

4. Now lead students in constructing a list of indirect characterization methods. They should come up with something like the following:

INDIRECT CHARACTERIZATION

The audience/reader makes judgments about a character's personality based on the following:

- The character's appearance
- The character's speech
- The character's actions
- What other characters say about him

---

5. Now lead students to define direct characterization. Explain that this method was not used in the skits. They should be able to come up with something like the following:

DIRECT CHARACTERIZATION

The author tells the audience/reader directly what the character is like. We don't have to guess.

---

6. Help students understand that plays, television shows, and movies rely mainly on indirect characterization. We watch the characters interact and form opinions about them. (However, a trend in movies and television today is to use direct characterization through what is called a "voice-over," with a narrator's voice giving details of the story or background information.)

Since we believe more of what we see than what we are told, indirect characterization is a very important tool in helping an author show a character. Authors are much more effective when they *show*, rather than *tell*.

DIALOGUE BANTER

»INDIRECT CHARACTERIZATION IS DEVELOPED through the character's speech, the character's actions, the character's appearance, and the character's interactions with others. This exercise concentrates on the importance of a character's *speech* in developing character.

Show or read aloud this conversation as an example:

"Do you know why I stopped you?"

"I have no idea."

"Could you please hand me your license and registration?"

"Oh, no! I left my purse at home! Here's the registration. My license is in my purse."

"Could you please step out of the car?"

"Do I have to? I want to call my mom."

"Put your hands where I can see them! Get out of the car now! Put your hands of the top of the car!"

"I'm trying! Please d-d-d-on't hurt me!

It seems pretty obvious that the characters in the above dialogue are a police officer and a young female driver. The officer seems a bit overzealous and the teen seems afraid. This information can be surmised from the speech of the characters alone.

Explain that students will now work in pairs to write their own dialogue. The class will then draw conclusions about who the characters are, why they are acting the way they are, what they are feeling, etc.

PROCEDURE

1. Make a copy of the opening lines on page 40. Cut the opening lines into strips. (Because the class will be divided into pairs, you need half the number of students in your class.)

2. Divide the class into pairs and have each pair draw a strip with an opening line.

3. Explain that each opening line becomes the beginning of a dialogue for "character one." The second person responds to the line as "character two." The students pass the paper back and forth to create a conversation. Each person should write a minimum of eight lines; therefore the dialogue will be at least sixteen lines long.

(continued)

Each pair of students writes one dialogue. The pair may decide in the beginning who the two people are, or they may let the dialogue evolve on its own. You will be amazed at the students' creativity, and students should be able to see the importance of dialogue in developing character.

4. When the dialogues are complete, each pair goes to the front and reads aloud. At the close of each dialogue, ask the class these questions:

•   Who are the two people?
•   How can you tell?
•   Why are they reacting as they are?
•   What can you tell about their personalities?

Here is a student example:

1: What did you say he looks like?

2: I didn't say. I said he's funny.

1: Sooo, he isn't cute.

2: Why can't a guy be funny *and* cute? You are so superficial.

1: If he's so funny and cute, why don't you go out with him?

2: He's not my type.

1: And your type is what, exactly?

2: Smart, handsome, rich, and funny.

1: So this friend is funny, but not smart or handsome or rich?

2: Do you want a date to homecoming, or not? He's the best I can do.

1: What did you tell him about me?

2: I said you were funny!

1: Great! So now he thinks I'm ugly or fat!

2: You are ugly and fat!

1: I can't believe you just said that!

2: You know I'm just kidding. Anyway, guys don't ask that sort of thing. He doesn't care what you look like. He's willing to take you if you double with John and me. He needs a date, you are desperate for a date, it's only a week away...

1: So how do I meet him?

2: Well, he's coming this way! See, over there.

1: He's gorgeous! But wait! Is he walking with a cane?

2: What did you expect? You said you wanted a blind date!

(continued)

DIALOGUE BANTER

OPENING LINES

1. How old is this?

2. I need you to concentrate.

3. It's cold in here.

4. You call this clean?

5. It's ten minutes past your curfew.

6. My daddy says...

7. Where were you last night?

8. Cut the blue wire.

9. It was here a minute ago.

10. What did you say he looks like?

11. How fast can this thing go?

12. Who wants to go to the circus?

13. I'm sorry. I have to wash my hair.

14. I just want to be friends.

15. Is your mother home?

16. Please step on the scale.

17. Do you know why I stopped you?

18. I hate it when you act this way!

19. Have we met?

20. You are not my mother!

21. Whoa! What was that?!

22. Is she breathing?

23. I think they forgot about us.

24. What size do you wear?

25. When did you first notice the symptoms?

VOILA! CONVERT A STORY TO A PLAY

»READING ALOUD A SHORT STORY or passage from a novel can be tedious when the teacher calls on slow or unenthusiastic readers. But students love to read plays aloud. Try choosing several passages from a story and having students convert them to a play as they read. Reading is shared, so no one gets tired, and the story advances more quickly. Students also get practice in determining what is narration and what is dialogue.

Famous scenes to read aloud might be the court scene from *To Kill a Mockingbird* or *A Separate Peace*, the deathbed scene from *Wuthering Heights*, the torture scene from *1984*, etc. But this process will work with any novel or short story.

This process works best if you select a passage that contains a great deal of dialogue. Assign a part for each character and a narrator.

Tell the students to imagine the selected passage is a play, but the character identification is left off. Therefore, they have to figure out when to read, based on punctuation marks and paragraphing. Each character reads aloud the actual dialogue for that character. The narrator reads aloud the whole narrative sentences. (The "he says" and "she says" can be skipped.)

EXAMPLE

For this scene, from Mark Twain's *The Adventures of Tom Sawyer*, the teacher would assign the roles of *narrator, Tom,* and *Becky*. Here is the original scene:

Now Tom began to scrawl something on the slate, hiding the words from the girl. But she was not backward this time. She begged to see. Tom said:

"Oh, it ain't anything."

"Yes it is."

"No it ain't. You don't want to see."

"Yes I do, indeed I do. Please let me."

"You'll tell."

"No I won't—deed and deed and double deed won't."

"You won't tell anybody at all? Ever, as long as you live?"

"No, I won't ever tell ANYbody. Now let me."

"Oh, YOU don't want to see!"

"Now that you treat me so, I WILL see." And she put her small hand upon his and a little scuffle ensued, Tom pretending to resist in earnest but letting his hand slip by degrees till these words were revealed: "I LOVE YOU."

(continued)

VOILA! CONVERT A STORY TO A PLAY

"Oh, you bad thing!" And she hit his hand a smart rap, but reddened and looked pleased, nevertheless.

To convert the passage to a play, students would "rewrite" it verbally as they read it aloud. It would read as follows:

NARRATOR: Now Tom began to scrawl something on the slate, hiding the words from the girl. But she was not backward this time. She begged to see.

TOM: Oh, it ain't anything.

BECKY: Yes it is.

TOM: No it ain't. You don't want to see.

BECKY: Yes I do, indeed I do. Please let me.

TOM: You'll tell.

BECKY: No I won't—deed and deed and double deed won't.

TOM: You won't tell anybody at all? Ever, as long as you live?

BECKY: No, I won't ever tell ANYbody. Now let me.

TOM: Oh, YOU don't want to see!

BECKY: Now that you treat me so, I WILL see.

NARRATOR: And she put her small hand upon his and a little scuffle ensued, Tom pretending to resist in earnest but letting his hand slip by degrees till these words were revealed: I LOVE YOU.

BECKY: Oh, you bad thing!

NARRATOR: And she hit his hand a smart rap, but reddened and looked pleased, nevertheless.

SUSPENSE SCENE

»AUTHORS WANT TO HOOK READERS so that they will keep on reading. They do this by creating tension. People tend to feel anxiety or apprehension about uncertain, undecided, or mysterious situations. This tension or anxiety is called *suspense*.

Authors create suspense by using many of the following techniques:

1. The main character senses **a problem that needs to be solved.**
2. As the action rises, the character must decide between at least **two major choices.**
3. **Sensory details** help create an air of mystery or danger.
4. An **evil villain** helps propel action.
5. A **time deadline** creates tension.
6. **Moments of doubt** confuse the character.
7. **Time seems to slow down** at a crucial point.
8. **New aspects of the problem** surprise the character.
9. **Helplessness** paralyzes the character for a period of time.
10. Dramatic irony—**we know something the character doesn't**—is added.

Using some of the techniques above, create a suspenseful scene based on one of the following lines:

1. No one knew where the knife landed.
2. When I entered the house, I heard a strange noise coming from the corner.
3. None of us was really sure what went on at that neighbor's house.
4. I opened the door, but no one was there.
5. I'll never forget that scream as long as I live.

FOR FURTHER EXPLORATION

Watch a suspenseful movie and determine which elements of suspense from the above list were used. Give specific examples from the movie.

CHARACTER MEMORY BOX

»SOME MEMORIES ARE SO PRECIOUS that they deserve to be kept in a special place, a place like a memory box. Memory boxes are typically made of wood and contain memorabilia from a person's life.

Making a memory box is like making a three dimensional scrapbook. The owner collects objects that hold particular memories of places and people in his or her life. Typical contents might be photographs, small objects, ticket stubs, letters, postcards, fabric, jewelry, and other souvenirs. The objects help the owner remember the sight, sound, smell, taste, and touch of past events. Memory boxes may be made to commemorate special events such as weddings, births, a deceased person's life, family traditions, etc. Some companies even specialize in selling memory boxes.

ASSIGNMENT

1. For this activity, you will select a character from one of the novels or short stories we have read this year and construct that character's memory box. The box may be made of wood, cardboard (a shoebox, for example), tin, or whatever you like. The box should be decorated to make it look attractive. Decorate your box with paints, markers, paper, wallpaper, string, glitter, buttons, etc. It should be something the character would be proud of.

2. Then place in the box at least five items that would be important to that character. (Use no more than one photo.) Write an explanation of each item and quote the part of the story that supports your explanation.

3. When called upon, share your memory box with the class.

CHARACTER PRESS CONFERENCE

»THIS ACTIVITY CAN BE USED AS A CULMINATING activity after students read a novel, short story, or play.

Assign several students in the class to "become" the characters in a novel. They are to be seated in chairs in the front of the class. Members of the class are reporters. Each member writes down two questions to ask the characters. The characters answer based on events that happened in the book and the type of person the character seems to be. Questions might include something like the following:

- Why did you...?

- What did you think would happen when you...?

- When did you first realize...?

- How do you justify...?

- How did you feel about...?

This process forces students to think about character motives and background.

After the character interviews, lead a discussion about the validity of the answers given. Was any of the information contradictory to information given in the story? Did any of the characters lie? Why or why not? How do you know? What insights into the characters emerged?

WRITING POETRY

Activities that Unleash Creativity

WRITERS DEFINE POETRY

»**BEFORE SHOWING THE DEFINITIONS BELOW,** ask students to define poetry. Have them write down what they know in a half page. At first many will think that they know nothing, but after they start writing, they will usually find that they know more than they think.

Then have students share, and write a list of their ideas on the board. They are likely to list rhythm, rhyme, free verse, alliteration, simile, metaphor, haiku, the names of some poems they have read, names of famous poets, etc.

Next show them what writers themselves say about poetry. Share the quotations below and ask students to discuss them. Do they agree or disagree with what the poet says? The quotations usually promote a deep and lively discussion.

1. Prose—words in their best order; poetry—the best words in their best order. (Samuel Taylor Coleridge)

2. Poetry comes with anger, hunger, and dismay; it does not often visit groups of citizens sitting down to be literary together, and would appall them if it did. (Christopher Morley)

3. Painting is silent poetry, and poetry is painting that speaks. (Attributed to Simonides by Plutarch)

4. Poetry is the language in which man explores his own amazement. (Christopher Fry)

5. If I read a book and it makes my whole body so cold no fire can ever warm me, I know *that* is poetry. If I feel physically as if the top of my head were taken off, I know *that* is poetry. These are the only ways I know. Is there any other way? (Emily Dickinson)

6. It is easier to write a mediocre poem than to understand a good one. (Michel de Montaigne)

7. A poet puts the world into a nutshell; the orator, out of a nutshell, brings a world. (James Hurnard)

8. Who writes poetry imbibes honey from the poisoned lips of life. (William Rose Benet)

(continued)

WRITERS DEFINE POETRY

9. Poets utter great and wise things which they do not themselves understand. (Pluto)

10. As far as I am concerned, that is as good a definition as can be given of a poet: that he is one who feels the world as a gift. (James Dickey)

11. Modern poets are bells of lead. They should tinkle melodiously but usually they just klunk. (Lord Dunsany)

12. I sound my barbaric yawp over the roofs of the world. (Walt Whitman)

13. To have great poets, there must be great audiences, too. (Walt Whitman)

14. The strongest and sweetest songs yet remain to be sung. (Walt Whitman)

Finally, have students write their *own* poetic definitions of poetry to share with the class. Here are a few examples students have come up with in the past:

- Poetry is liquid emotion set on fire.

- Poetry is the cry of the heart from the deep recesses of the soul.

- Poetry is the rhythm of the dance of life.

- A poem is the hush which quiets the crowd just before the winner is announced.

- Poetry gives birth to the revelation of mankind's inner spirit.

LIQUID IMAGINATION

»SOMETIMES STUDENT WRITERS EXPERIENCE WRITER'S BLOCK. This activity will free the mind to flow creatively and think poetically.

1. To begin the activity, put a word on the board (*red* or *mirror*, for example.) You may choose the word or let the students choose the word. Explain that students have one minute to list as many words as possible that flow from the first word. They may write opposites, synonyms, or anything they like. They may include single words or phrases.

2. At the end of one minute, have the students count how many words they have listed. Twenty or more is good; fewer means the writer needs to learn to let go and not self-edit.

3. Explain to the class that our imaginations are like liquid. A liquid spilled on a flat surface will flow in all directions until stopped by an obstacle. Our imaginations tend to flow in somewhat the same manner; one word suggests another, which suggests another, which suggests another.

    Ask students to look at their lists as though another person is looking at them, putting an asterisk anywhere that the list seems to jump, anywhere the flow might not make sense to someone else. The writer might be able to explain the connection, but another person would just see a jump. These jumps are where the person has introduced an obstacle and caused the flow to go another way.

    For example, the writer may have written, "red...rose...love...grave." "Grave" seems like a jump to someone reading the list, but the writer knows he was thinking about how he placed a red rose on the grave of a loved one who died.

4. Allow volunteers to read their lists aloud. We often learn volumes about each other through this activity, especially as volunteers explain their imagination jumps.

5. Repeat the activity as many times as you wish. Students should write more and more freely each time, with more and more words each time.

6. Now ask students to look at their "jumps" and choose one idea as the basis for a poem of at least eight lines.

(continued)

LIQUID IMAGINATION

Here is a student example of a poem written from the brainstorm list that started with *mirror*:

MASKED

She lies motionless on her bed.
Her tangled hair is strewn across her pillow.
An empty tissue box sits on the floor,
Its former contents filling up the wastebasket.

Her face, buried in her hands, is red and hot;
Mascara is smeared under her eyes
And on the tops of her cheeks.

A muffled sigh escapes her sore throat,
Followed by a weak sniff.
She sits up, tired, eyes red, breathing softly.
Staring blankly she pauses for a moment, thinking.

She pulls out a mirror and wipes away the mascara
And still damp tears from her face,
Hiding all the evidence.
Oh, what would people think of her?
She gathers herself,
Gives one last deep sigh,
And returns to her masked life.

Jenna Squyres

PICTURE REFLECTIONS

»THIS ACTIVITY HELPS STUDENTS FEEL SAFE to write and share ideas.

MATERIALS NEEDED. You will need ten to fifteen pictures to post and three colors of sticky notes per student. Find ten to fifteen pictures that seem to mirror different emotions. Pictures can be found in magazines, old calendars, on posters, or on the Internet under different picture categories.

PROCEDURE

1. Show your students the pictures and ask them to come to some consensus about what emotion, feeling, or character trait each picture represents. For example, my students decided that a picture of a jar filled with lightning bugs represented creative ideas or creativity. A prisoner looking out of bars represented feeling trapped. Children standing on their heads represented playfulness.

2. Now tape the pictures across the top of the chalkboard and assign each a number, one to fifteen. Give each student three sticky notes in different colors—one color to represent a student's *always* self, one color to represent a student's *sometimes* self, and one color to represent a student's *never* self. I used green sticky notes for *always*, yellow sticky notes for *sometimes*, and red sticky notes for *never* (kind of like a traffic light).

3. Each student then chooses three of the fifteen pictures—one to represent his or her *always* self, one to represent his *sometimes* self, and one to represent his *never* self. For example, I might say that my *always* self (green) is the picture with the lightning bugs because I am always full of ideas; my *sometimes* self (yellow) might be the picture of the children standing on their heads because I enjoy life; my *never* self (red) might be the picture of the trapped person because I feel free to follow my passions. I would write my name on each sticky note along with the number of the picture I chose for each category.

4. Have students take turns going to the board and placing their sticky notes under the pictures they chose. They should explain to the class why they chose each picture.

5. After all have posted their sticky notes, discuss which picture attracted the most response in each category. Then ask students to write a three-stanza poem that describes their *always* self, *sometimes* self, and *never* self. Students don't necessarily have to use those words in their poems, but the categories should be apparent.

FREE VERSE POEMS

»**FREE VERSE IS POETRY WRITTEN WITHOUT RULES** about form, rhyme, rhythm, meter, etc. In free verse the writer makes his own rules. The writer decides how the poem should look, feel, and sound. Free verse can be a great way to express what a person really feels. This exercise helps students learn to write free verse poetry.

1. Display the following two poems, copying them exactly as written below. Ask students to copy them.

   I never saw a wild thing sorry for itself a small bird will drop frozen dead from a bough without ever having felt sorry for itself

   On a flat road runs the well-trained runner he is lean and sinewy with muscular legs he is thinly clothed he leans forward as he runs with lightly closed fists and arms partially raised

2. Divide students into groups of four. Each group is to decide how to arrange the two poems on the page as a free verse poem. They may break the lines wherever they like. They may elect to use punctuation or omit it; however, if they decide to use punctuation, it should be used correctly and consistently throughout the poem. They may begin each line with a capital letter, only capitalize the beginning of each sentence, or omit capital letters altogether. Each poem may be written in one or more stanzas.

3. Each group then displays its poem, using a transparency, the chalkboard, or a computer projector. Group members explain why they wrote each poem in the manner they chose.

4. After each group has presented, show the students the way each poem was actually written by the poet (next page).

(continued)

SELF-PITY

I never saw a wild thing
sorry for itself.
A small bird will drop frozen dead from a bough
without ever having felt sorry for itself.

D.H. Lawrence

THE RUNNER

On a flat road runs the well-trained runner,
He is lean and sinewy with muscular legs,
He is thinly clothed, he leans forward as he runs,
With lightly closed fists and arms partially raised.

Walt Whitman

Other possible poems that would work well for this exercise are "Fog" by Carl Sandburg and "Glimpse of Night" by Frank Marshall Davis.

FOLLOW-UP. Ask students to find articles in magazines that interest them. Then have them choose one short paragraph from an article and write it as a free verse poem. Students then present their poems to the class.

Here is an example. This poem is made from part of the opening paragraph of "The Politeness Project," by Holly Robinson (*Ladies' Home Journal*, April 2010, page 52).

Recently
three people were rude to me
in as many hours.

First a bank teller shrugged
and snapped her gum
when I asked why she put a hold
on my paycheck.

Then a teenager whizzed by
on a skateboard
and nearly knocked me flat.

Finally, at lunch,
the waitress forgot my order.
After I reminded her,
she brought me cold soup
and shoved it in front of me
without a word.

(continued)

FREE VERSE POEMS

This poem is made from part of the opening paragraph of "Mom Time," by Amy Beal (*Parenting*, April 2010, page 23.)

The kids are fighting,
dinner's burning
and the cat just booted
on the new rug—again.

Instead of sticking your head
in the oven, take three deep breaths,
concentrating only on the air
moving in and out of your nose...

Pop a Life Saver into your mouth.
Focus on the fruity taste of the cherry
lime
orange
or pineapple flavor
and resist the temptation to chew.

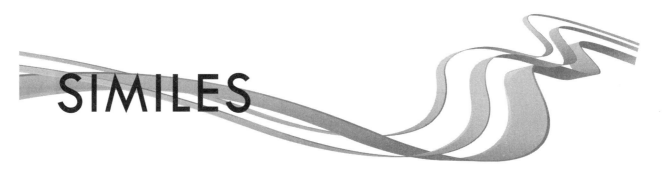

SIMILES

»A SIMILE IS A COMPARISON between two unlike things using the words *like* or *as*. Here are some examples:

- Her bangs looked like broken spokes in a wagon wheel.

- Her face is like cold steel, unyielding and unemotional.

- The scream pierced like a splinter under a fingernail.

- She is as pretty as a pumpkin pie on a Thanksgiving table.

- The room was as cold as an executioner's heart.

- His hair looked like fishing worms crawling in a cup.

- The material felt as soft as an overripe peach.

- The snow looked like powdered sugar beignets at Café Du Monde in New Orleans.

Complete the following lines with original similes. Do not use a trite comparison like "pretty as a picture" or "cold as ice." Try to think of something that no one else in the class will write.

1. The pencil sharpener sounded like...

2. The baby's face looked like...

3. The whistle of the train sounded like...

4. His arms were as _____ as _____.

5. The bells were as _____ as _____.

6. The canyon looked like...

7. The dress fit like...

8. The words pierced like...

9. The child's eyes were like...

10. The door squeaked like...

Now write a poem of eight lines or longer containing at least one simile. You may write a rhyming poem or a free verse poem. You may want to start with one of the similes you wrote in class and expand it into a poem by explaining your comparison. Or think of important people in your life (mother, father, sisters, brothers, friends, etc.) and compare them to something else, using one person for each stanza.

(continued)

SIMILES

EXAMPLE

My mother is like a stun gun.
She never lets me have any fun.
Whenever I sit to watch TV,
She always tries to energize me.

My father is like a city bank
He... (etc.)

These student examples may give you some more ideas:

BODY PARTS

My hair is like a blanket made of silk that's
    soft to touch.
My ears are like my satellite, but they don't
    listen much.
My nose is like a button that is too big for my
    blouse.
My feet are like Godzilla—big enough to
    crush a house.

My shoulders are like plates holding more
    than I can chew.
My mind is like a scrapbook full of
    photographs of you.
My soul is like a bird that's ready to fly away.
And my heart is like an empty home where
    no one wants to stay.

Allison Myers

AW...

You're like my sweater in October
And my Lucky Charms in the morning.

You're like the polyester in my favorite pants
And an episode of UCB.

You're like my Dr Pepper after school
And the duct tape on my backpack.

You're like the fortune in my cookie
And the icing on my cake.

But you can be anything you want to be.
I'll like you just the same.

Stevi Huggins

STAR

I caught a star
On my tongue.
It was quite hot
Like a fireball

Or a hot tamale.
Maybe we should
Put it in food
To spice things up.

Jared Harper

METAPHORS

»A METAPHOR IS A COMPARISON between two unlike things without using the words *like* or *as*. The writer simply states that one thing *is* something else or implies the comparison. A few examples:

- Success is the last piece placed in a 500-piece puzzle.

- Loneliness is an empty box of Cracker-Jack after the circus leaves.

- Parents are ladders that lift their children to platforms of success.

- Failure is a kite-eating tree.

- Diamonds are the sparkling eyes of Mother Nature.

- The jewelry box was filled with broken pieces of a lost relationship.

- School is a potter's wheel where lumps of clay are molded into beautiful works of art.

Complete the following metaphors. Be original. Try to think of something that no one else in the class will write. Use a noun, not an *ing* word for the metaphor.

No: Love is apologizing for something you didn't do.
Yes: Love is an unexpected apology.

1. Money is ...

2. A fortune cookie is...

3. Lemons are...

4. A button is...

5. Freedom is...

6. Anger is...

7. A mother is...

8. Memories are...

9. Truth is...

10. Waves are...

11. You choose...

12. You choose...

(continued)

METAPHORS

Now write a poem of eight lines or longer containing at least one metaphor. You may write a rhyming poem or a free verse poem. You may want to start with one of the metaphors you wrote in class and expand it into a poem by explaining your comparison. Another idea would be to think of comparisons that illustrate different moods. You might start with, "Yesterday I was _____." The next stanza could be "Today I am _____." Here's an example:

> Yesterday I was water just before it boils,
> A rubber band stretched almost to the limit,
> A popcorn kernel right before it bursts, and
> A paratrooper just about to jump.
>
> Today I am Saturday morning with no alarm,
> A quiet lake on a summer day,
> A sleeping baby in her mother's arms, and
> A cup of coffee with a chocolate dessert.

These student examples may give you some more ideas:

I LOVE

I'll be the love song
That has no end.
I'll be the melody
That warms your heart.
I'll be the notes
So soft and smooth.
I'll be the beat
That makes you move.
I'll be the masterpiece
That brings you joy.
I'll be the phonograph
That plays your favorite tune.
I'll be everything you need me to be.
I'll be your all. Just wait and see.

Brittany Rosario

PLASTIC

You are pieces of plastic
Carefully molded for the soul intent
Of complimenting my form and style.

You are the Tupperware container
And I am the stew.
I am carefully placed
Within your care, because I know
You will follow through.
You will hold me tight and
Never let me go.

Monique Perry

IMAGE POEMS

»EXPLAIN TO STUDENTS THAT THEY WILL WRITE DOWN IMAGES that are created in their minds in response to the words you will read. They should number the items, writing down the prompt word and then writing a brief description of the picture or object they "see." Students should answer quickly, writing down their first idea without taking time to self-edit. Possible responses to "home," for example, might be "homemade cookies" or "remote control battles" or simply "Mom."

WORD LIST

1. home
2. chaos
3. happiness
4. hope
5. mother
6. poverty
7. fear
8. loneliness
9. death
10. romance
11. wealth
12. silence
13. anger
14. hurt
15. joy

Now have the students read out their responses for each word, going down the rows quickly. Some may pass if they write something personal (for example, writing "stepmother" as the image they see for "death").

After sharing the responses, ask students to expand one or two of the images into poems of at least eight lines. Most of the poems will be extended metaphors.

See student examples on the following page.

(continued)

IMAGE POETRY

SILENCE CAN BE VIOLENT

Silence can be violent
It can tear into your core
To where you've become so numb
That pain doesn't hurt anymore
The simplicity is deteriorating
The truth has died
All you have is nothing
Nothing can be left to hide
Traces of the past can haunt you
Fearing the unknown is wise
Twisting up the story
Covering up the truth
Leaving nothing behind
But lies and deception
Breaking down into your soul
Tearing at you piece by piece
Silence can be violent
Unknown
Feared

Chrissi Brannin

HURT

The walls of my soul have been hole-
punched.
My fears are leaking out.
Tears and scars and memories hurt the most.
I don't have a safety net.
Don't ask me what's wrong.
I'm just not okay.

Kelly Hammock

DEATH

Death is a black rose, a final good-bye,
A single moment captured in time,
The memory of the life that passes you by.

Death is final judgment of all things not confessed,
A strong feeling of overwhelming sadness,
The certainty of knowing you didn't do your best.

Death is darkness that sneaks up from behind.
It's everything unknown, silent, and sly.
It possesses your body and takes over your mind.

Brittany Rosario

PERSONIFICATION

»**PERSONIFICATION IS LANGUAGE** that gives human characteristics to inanimate objects or abstract ideas. Some examples:

- The raindrops kissed my face.
- The road beckoned me to follow.
- My mother's quilt hugged me with her love.

Complete each of the following with an original personification. Try to think of something that no one else in the class will write.

1. The car

2. The computer

3. The warm sun

4. The moon

5. The paper clip

6. Fire

7. The window of the old house

8. The rain

9. Anger

10. The tree

11. Your choice

12. Your choice

Now expand one of your ideas into a poem of at least eight lines. See examples on following page.

(continued)

PERSONIFICATION

I AM A TREE

I am a tree.
The wind blows softly
in my hair.
Baby birds in their nests
rest on my shoulders.
I breathe air for people
and make shade.
They come to me after
working all day
in the
hot
desert sun.
I comfort them
In my arms.
Then
they rest.

Bobby Nation

DEATH

We strain our eyes and minds,
Searching for life after life
As we near the borders of our lives.
Death touches my face
Burning my skin with frozen fingers,
Not quite taking me or embracing me.
My eyes sting as I
Search for life after life
As we reach the borders of our lives.

Micah Baham

PROVERB POEM

Home is where the forest is
And blackberries frolic and play
Pine needles dance upon the leaves
The mother wind whispers in your ear

And purple clouds let raindrops fall
Telling stories from yesterday
The birds sing the song
You wish you knew
Of the forest from far away

Mariah Gilbert

THE DARKNESS INSIDE

It crawls on the ceiling.
It crawls on the walls.
It seeps through the windows.
It follows me in the halls.

Inside my body,
All through my head,
It eats in my kitchen.
It sleeps in my bed.

Please go away.
Stop following me around.
The darkness inside of me,
To its walls, I am bound.

This darkness is evil.
I feel it all times.
It slowly makes me
Lose my mind.

Kristin Chandler

ONOMATOPOEIA POEMS

»**ONOMATOPOEIA** is the use of words that imitate sounds, such as *bang, whisper, whoosh, sizzle,* or any word whose sound is suggestive of its meaning.

Play a piece of music that suggests many sounds. The music should be free of lyrics and perhaps use many different instruments, including drums. Walt Disney's *The Jungle Book* soundtrack songs "Tiger Fight" and "What'cha Wanna Do" are two songs that work well. The students write the sounds they hear, spelling them phonetically. Students may come up with words like *rat-a-tat, zizzer, zig, sizzle, boom, thud, plop, ripit, teep-teep,* etc.

Ask several students to share their lists. Then ask students to write a poem of at least eight lines containing a minimum of three examples of onomatopoeia.

Here are some examples by students.

MORNING

Zah! Zah! The alarm clock rings.
Phrum! Phrum! The awakened girl sings.
Kerplunk! The bird flaps its wings.
Flap, flap! The bird flies away.
Wa, wa! The baby starts to say.
Ching, ching! The girl gets her pay.
Zzzz! Zzzz! The girl ends her day.

Emily Spencer

MY GUITAR

My guitar,
blaring, screaming, and twanging,
raging solos, ringing rhythmic notes,
loud songs
through my amplifier.
Creating great vibes throughout my room.
Not stopping between bloodcurdling cries,
even to take a breath.

Bobby Nation

BEAUTIFUL EVENING

The birds chirp chirped.
The bees buzz buzzed.
The wind blew ever so gently with a
whoosh.
The trees danced and rustled their leaves.
The sun was setting.
I sighed an "ah."
Drip, drip, wish; the rain fell gently.
What a beautiful evening.

Kristin Chandler

ALLITERATION POEM

»**ALLITERATION IS A FREQUENTLY USED POETIC DEVICE** in which initial consonant sounds in two or more neighboring words or syllables are repeated. After discussing alliteration with your students, divide the class into groups of four. Each group then writes an alliterative sentence about the other members of the group and one about himself or herself.

Alliteration sentences may contain some truth, but students should be encouraged to write zany or outrageous (but not insulting) sentences. Groups should then share sentences with each other and select one sentence for each member to be included in a class poem. The teacher collects all the sentences and combines them to make a class alliteration poem.

Here is an example of one poem written by a class:

PEOPLE POEM

Creative writing creates crazy kids:

Katie complains kinky curls can't comb straight.

Tim takes time to tell the tale.

Kristin keeps kooky kids in line.

Brandon's big, bad, bodacious, bald head
    babbles on about blood, brains, and beetles.

Amanda always awkwardly answers Andy.

Kaylene cuts coupons for cabbage.

Angela willingly dumped Will on Wednesday.

Kristi cautiously crosses the creek to climb the cliff.

Karla's kinda kooky when she kisses kangaroos.

When Mary moos, many men want to meet her.

Dana Chesser chimes and chirps.

Chelsea chomps chicken cheerfully.

Sunni has a sugar-sweet sunshine smile.

Cassidy colors with crazy crayons in the coloring book of
    cantaloupes.

Angela argues about awfully obnoxious guys.

Crazy kids create creative writing!

EKPHRASTIC POEMS

»EKPHRASTIC POETRY IS POETRY COMPOSED IN RESPONSE to a piece of art—a painting, photograph, sculpture, or a piece of music, for example. In essence, one form of art is converted to another form of art. The instructions below are for poems created in response to a painting or photograph.

PROCEDURE

1. Select a painting or drawing to share with the class. Posters of famous paintings or pictures from the Internet work well. Or even better, take a field trip to a local museum.

2. Have students brainstorm at least ten questions about the picture. (Who are the people shown? What is the setting? Is it in the past, present, or future? Why does the painting use only two primary colors? What is the mood of the picture? What is that in the corner? etc.)

3. Ask students to share their questions with the class. Many will notice details others missed.

4. Then have students write a poem about the picture. The poem may be rhymed or free verse and must be at least twelve lines long.

5. Allow students to read their poems aloud and then display the poems on a bulletin board along with the picture.

This poem was written in response to Pablo Picasso's painting *Woman Ironing*.

WOMAN IRONING

All by herself
She works through the day
To iron her clothes
And put the wrinkles away.
She lays them out straight,
But the wrinkles come back.
They soon become clothes
Just thrown in a stack.
Five times she irons them,
Sometimes ten.

But somehow the wrinkles
Come back again.
Soon though she realizes
It's just part of life
To have wrinkles and tears,
To have beauty and strife.
For nothing is perfect.
Our wrinkles we see,
But sometimes we have
To just let them be.

Adrienne Seal

MUSIC POEMS

»IMAGERY INVOLVES LANGUAGE THAT CREATES in the reader's mind mental images or emotions that appeal to the five senses—especially sight, but also hearing, taste, touch, and smell. After discussing imagery with your students, have them write their own imagery in response to music.

PROCEDURE

1. Select a piece of music that creates a mood and contains no lyrics.

2. Explain that you will play the chosen selection for students while they close their eyes and imagine what might be happening if this music were the background music for a movie. What would they see, hear, taste, feel, smell?

3. Play the music again and ask students to write whatever comes into their minds. It might be a list, a story, a description, etc.

4. Give each student a blank sheet of paper and ask each to "draw" the music.

5. Finally, using their drawing and what they have already written as inspiration, ask students to write a poem of at least eight lines about the music.

6. Have students share their poems and pictures with the class.

Classical and jazz music or movie soundtracks work very well for this activity. I have used "Respect the Wind" from the *Twister* soundtrack and "This Begins Our Broadcast Day" from the *Cable Guy* soundtrack.

For a sample music poem, see the following page.

(continued)

THE AWAKENING

Sleeping Beauty awakes.
She can't remember where she is.
Eyes twitch, flutter, open.
In a casket.
Sit up; the world in age.
Vines cascade down walls.
At her glance, they blossom.
She arises, walks around, glides.
Life returns at her touch.
Sleeping people awake.
Life, movement, rebirth!
Energy, strength, light.
Now moving, spreading—
At first a trickle,
Then a stream,
Now a flood.
Everywhere, newness, life.
Radiant energy and finally—
Joy!

Ann Barr

OBJECT POEMS

»THIS ACTIVITY HELPS STUDENTS understand how objects can be used to symbolize a quality, idea, lesson, etc.

PROCEDURE

1. Ask students to choose an object that connects them to the past. For example, they might choose a toy or an item of clothing. Have them consider what the object has experienced, taught, learned, expressed, caused, etc.

2. Students then write a poem of at least eight lines about the object. They might tell what the object has to teach, what quality the object has that they need, what memories the object brings, etc.

3. After some students share their poems, point out how they have just used symbolism, whether they realized it or not. Discuss how symbolism is often used in literature, and ask students to think of some examples.

   Here are some examples of student object poems:

THE TEDDY BEAR PENNY

When I was little
My brother gave me a penny
With a Teddy Bear on it.
He said,
"When you miss me,
Just look at this penny,
And I'll be there."
I looked up at him.
I felt like I was the richest person alive,
And yet,
It was only a penny.

Caleb Carlyle

TIME

As I sit here
Watching the seconds of my life
Tick away, I realize how much
My life has sunk into the deep pits
Of despair; how much I've fallen
Into a state of apathetic loneliness
Where I hear only the
Incessant ticking of time.

Micah Baham

Another example may be found in the Appendix on page 143.

LIST POEMS

»SOMETIMES A POET CREATES A POEM by writing a list. The list may contain figurative language or other poetic elements. Here are two examples:

MY CAR

My car is my office,
with laptop and printer
files and cell phone
and paper clips scattered on the floor.

My car is my home,
with sleeping bag and pillow
in the trunk,
a few changes of clothes,
dirty socks and two pairs of shoes
stuffed behind the seat,
a toothbrush, toothpaste,
and an extra razor in the glove box.
And there is a little fox puppet
in the back window in case I get lonely.

My car is my kitchen
with bags of pretzels and popcorn,
chocolate covered peanuts
and trail mix, apples and orange peels,
bottles of juice and tea and water,
many empty, some half full, all spilling out
from under the passenger seat.

My car is a small bookstore,
brimmingly filled with boxes of books,
cases of cassettes and CD's,
fliers and order forms,
a cash box, and credit card receipts.

My car is a small sound stage
complete with three microphones,
booms and mic stands,
miles of cables and cords,
speakers, amps, a tape player,
and a wireless transcender.

My car is my office, my home, my kitchen,
a bookstore, a soundstage and
a fiery chariot that carries me, a talespinner,
across the mythical realms
where the Brothers Grimm
live with Johnny Appleseed,
where Reynard the Fox
plays with Pan the Piper,
where listeners for a moment
lose their way in the dark wood
before finding the glistening pool
where they can pause
and reflect...

from *Song of the Red Fox* by Brian "Fox" Ellis
Copyright © 2003 Fox Tales International,
Peoria, Illinois. Used with permission

(continued)

LIST POEMS

excerpt from "Song of Myself"

A child said, what is the grass? fetching it to me with full hands;
How could I answer the child?...I do not know what it is any more than he.

I guess it must be the flag of my disposition, out of hopeful green
    stuff woven.

Or I guess it is the handkerchief of the Lord,
A scented gift and remembrancer designedly dropped,
Bearing the owner's name someway in the corners, that we may see
    and remark, and say *Whose?*

Or I guess the grass is itself a child, the produced babe of the vegetation.

Or I guess it is a uniform hieroglyphic,
And it means, Sprouting alike in broad zones and narrow zones,
Growing among black folks as among white,
Kanuck, Tuckahoe, Congressman, Cuff, I give them the same, I
    receive them the same.

And now it seems to me the beautiful uncut hair of graves.

Walt Whitman

WRITING ACTIVITY—SOLO

1. Ask students to describe a place, an object, or a feeling, writing their descriptions as a list and using as many details as they can.
2. After they have written their lists, have them go back over them, making changes and additions to include language that appeals to the senses. Ask them to shape their lists into free verse poems of at least eight lines.

WRITING ACTIVITY—GROUP

Divide the class into groups of four and send them to various locations on the school campus (front office, cafeteria, gym, hallway, restroom, band room, etc.). They will have fifteen minutes to take descriptive notes on their location. When they return to class, they write a list

(continued)

poem of at least twelve lines about the place they visited. (If sending the students out of class isn't an option at your school, the groups can do the same activity, writing about the classroom. Though they will be writing about the same location, the resulting poems are likely to be very different.)

Here are some examples of student list poems:

SOME DAYS

Some days you're the windshield,
Some days you're the bug.
Some days you're the baseball bat,
Some days you're the glove.
Some days you're the salt,
Some days you're the slug.
But all in all I would just rather be,
NONE of the above.

Claire Shidler

LET'S STEP OUTSIDE

Let's step outside...the room.
Let's step outside...the house.
Let's step outside...the neighborhood.
Let's step outside...the city.
Let's step outside...the state.
Let's step outside...the country.
Let's step outside...the continent.
Let's step outside...the world.
Let's step outside...the universe.
Let's step outside...together.

Brittany Hutches

CIRCUS IN MY HEAD

I have a circus in my head.
People are walking
On tightropes way up high.
Bears are balancing on balls.
Clowns ride in tiny cars.
Lions do stupid tricks.
People are flipping and
Riding on elephants.
There are monkeys on trampolines and
Ponies walking like people and
Giraffes skipping around and
Mimes in invisible boxes.
I have no idea why, but
One thing I know is
I hope this headache ends soon!

Rachel Glover

BORROWED LINE POETRY

»A GOOD WAY TO LEARN TO WRITE POETRY is to study the pros. With borrowed line poetry, students borrow a line from a famous poem or song and build something new around it.

PROCEDURE

1. Have students bring their favorite poems to class to share with others. (You might also want to allow song lyrics.)

2. As students listen to the poems, ask them to write down at least one line they like from each person's poem. Then ask several students to share the lines they chose.

3. The next step is for students to use one of the lines chosen, i.e., a "borrowed line," to compose a new poem of at least eight lines. Allow students to share their new poems with the rest of the class.

Here is one student example.

HOW DO I LOVE THEE?

How do I love thee? Let me count the ways...
I don't love you, so I can't really count them.
It's hard to even think about loving someone who bugs me so much.
And I know it's not entirely your fault,
But mostly it is.

I know you can't help all the annoying things you do,
But I really wish you could.
If I could just get past all your problems,
Maybe I could love you,
Or maybe not.
You're really not that bad,
When you're not talking, that is.
Otherwise, I really can't stand you.
Maybe someday you will find someone who can.
That person's just not me, and for that I am sorry,
But not really.

Jill Gibson

BAD COUNTRY BALLADS

»A BALLAD IS A POEM THAT TELLS A STORY. It is often sung and has a very musical quality. The theme is often tragic—a love gone bad—and it may contain dialogue or a refrain.

After you have read a few ballads together, have your students try writing their own, basing their ballads on bad country music song titles. The following is a list of supposedly real country song titles and/or first lines. (Some are real, but many likely originated as jokes or parts of other titles.) Copy these and cut them apart into strips.

Allow each student to draw a song title to use in writing a poem. The poem must be at least sixteen lines and tell a story. It may rhyme or be free verse.

For an example of a ballad based on a bad country song title, see next page.

1. How Can I Miss You If You Won't Go Away?

2. She Made Toothpicks out of the Timber of My Heart

3. How Could You Believe Me When I Said I Love You When You Know I've Been a Liar All My Life?

4. I Changed Her Oil, She Changed My Life

5. You're The Reason Our Kids Are Ugly

6. I Keep Forgettin' I Forgot about You

7. If My Nose Were Full of Nickels, I'd Blow It All on You

8. I'm Just a Bug on the Windshield of Life

9. Her Teeth Were Stained, but Her Heart Was Pure

10. When You Leave, Walk out Backwards, So I'll Think You're Walking In

11. If You Leave Me, Can I Come, Too?

12. Oh, I've Got Hair Oil on My Ears and My Glasses Are Slipping Down

13. My Wife Ran off with My Best Friend (And I Sure Do Miss Him)

14. Mama Get the Hammer (There's a Fly on Papa's Head)

15. They May Put Me in Prison, but They Can't Stop My Face from Breakin' Out

16. I Fell in a Pile of You and Got Love All over Me

(continued)

BAD COUNTRY BALLADS

17. If Love Were Oil, I'd Be About a Quart Low

18. You Can't Have Your Kate and Edith Too

19. You Were Only a Splinter As I Slid Down the Bannister of Life

20. You Done Stomped On My Heart (And Mashed That Sucker Flat)

21. I Wouldn't Take Her to a Dawg Fight, Cause I'm Afraid She'd Win

22. Here's a Quarter (Call Someone Who Cares)

23. Am I Double Parked by the Curbstone of Your Heart

24. You stuck My Heart in an Old Tin Can and Shot It Off a Log

25. Old Flames Can't Hold a Candle to You

26. I Bought the Boots That Just Walked Out on Me

27. I Sent Her Artificial Flowers for Her Artificial Love

28. Elvis Is Dead and I Don't Feel So Good Myself

29. The Only Ring You Gave Me Was the One Around the Tub

30. If I Ain't Got It, You Don't Need It

Here's a student example:

I CHANGED HER OIL, SHE CHANGED MY LIFE

She pulled up to the station
Doin' a Faith Hill imitation.
She wore cowboy boots and a Stetson hat,
And she drove her Chevy up to where I sat.
She had a blue tick hound just like mine.
Both of 'em together looked mighty fine.
She stepped out of the truck, and with a southern drawl
Said, "Excuse me, sir, could you change my oil?"
I said, "Yes, ma'am," and went to where she stood,
Pulled the switch, then opened the hood.
I looked at her and she looked at me.
Right then and there it was meant to be.
I changed her oil and that was that.
Then we both got under her Stetson hat.
It was paid in full by that big kiss.
That's one oil change I'll never forget.

Harmon Carson

COLOR POEMS

»**SIMPLE COLORS MAY BE SYMBOLIC,** depending on the context in which they are used. For example, a purple robe might symbolize royalty; a white bridal gown might symbolize purity; red might symbolize anger. People respond to colors in different ways, and the responses often take place on a subconscious, emotional level. Colors can evoke a mood, a feeling, or an emotion.

Divide the students into groups of four. Ask them to brainstorm what the colors black, red, white, and green often symbolize. Then have students share their ideas with the class.

WRITING

Ask students to write a color poem, using a single color at least three times in the poem, or they may use three different colors in the poem. The poem must be at least six lines long and may be either free verse or rhyming.

Here are some student examples:

ORANGE

Orange flames flash out across the sky.
You run and kick with the joy of being free.
You show off your orange physique.
Your hair flows with poise and grace.
Your thoroughbred heart beats fast.
You dance like the orange flames that burn
around you.
Your soul is on fire, forever free, with orange
flames
That dance throughout the sky.

Jordan Squyres

RED

The red blood taints
the water in the river
of your soul.

Crimson tears flow
from the eyes of my conscience
I caused you pain
and wept red rain.

Marlon Lampkin

See more examples on the following page.

(continued)

COLOR POEMS

BLACK

Black is the color of his heart
Matted and tangled in bundles of hatred
Black is the color of his soul
A soul that was once pure and loving
Fading into a darkness
Where even the brightest light refused to
shine.
Because to him it is nonexistent
Shame is all he ever knew
It lies in his heart
Hatred
The darkest shade of black.

Chrissi Brannan

BLUE

Once in a blue moon, your love is hotter
than a summer's most
miserable day
Once in a blue moon, you're cold as the winter's harshest snow
storm
Once in a blue moon, you break me beyond
all hope of
repair
But every night, blue, red, white, yellow, or
black, the
moon shines for you and me alone, and
angels envy our love
with green faces

Chris Fallin

WHITE

Wear your white
in the sea of black.
Dare to glow
in the room of darkness.
Be a bright white beacon
when all seems lost.
Dare to stand out.
Wear your white.

Carl Johnson

ORANGE

Orange, yellow, red
Like flame
Dancing down orange hallways
with flowing fire tapestries.
A red wolf stares at me
with yellow eyes
from the end of the corridor.
Through the halls
I chase him.
He's fast.
The fiery colors
dance around me
as I run
until finally I burst out
into the white outside
leaving my orange dream behind.
I wake up in my bed,
tangled in yellow sheets
and wonder where the wolf went

Amanda Rivers

ANSWERLESS QUESTIONS

»ASK STUDENTS TO CHOOSE ONE OF THE FOLLOWING QUESTIONS

and answer in the form of a free verse or rhyming poem of at least eight lines.

1. Which is colder, an iceberg or fear?

2. Which is itchier, a wool sweater or curiosity?

3. Which is softer, a kiss or cotton?

4. What shape is life?

5. What color is noise?

6. What is the taste of shame?

7. Which is warmer, love or the sun?

8. Which is more sour, a lemon or defeat?

9. Which is happier, sunrise or sunset?

10. What color is winning?

11. Which is slower, *K* or *Z?*

12. Which is heavier, an anvil or depression?

13. What color is success?

14. Which is more exciting, a roller coaster or love?

15. What causes you fear?

For student examples, see the following page.

(continued)

TEACHER FEAR

No other room could ever make me feel so caged.
Steel bars condemn our words, chairs lined
Row to row with each of us stoned by her speech.
Dead to conscious thought, we suffer.

Like a distraught tabby, I lick my wounds,
Festered with the salt she's poured.
The acid clings to my tongue; a poison in play.
My nerves dispel all feeling.
Malevolence grows in her, nurtured by her being.

Instructions, all imperative. A dictator, she waits as we
Follow the clues, read the lines one by one.
There is no gray for the indecisive.
Only black and white follow through, dominating our decisions.
Though our hope is there, it barely burns bright enough.

And it seems that time stops still to suit her schedule.
The minutes drudge by as if they were hours latched together
By the gossamer strands of years to pass.
As this wave of frozen faces bears towards her, we diminish.
Barely, we reach the height of her ankles on this coerced shore.

When all that's left are the days, the months;
The end seems all too far away to believe.
Inscribed on our memory, she stays.
No other room could ever make me feel so caged.

Ashley Lynch

SHAME

Can you taste your tongue
When you eat your shame?
Can you see your eyes
When you make them cry?
Can you hear your ears
When you tell the lies?
Can you touch your nerves
When you feel no love?
Dead mother, give me guidance from above.

Rafael Doolittle

PROGRESSIVE POETRY

»PROGRESSIVE POETRY MAY BE USED as an introduction to poetry or as a culminating activity. You may specify that the students use certain poetic devices in writing the poems, or you may let them decide for themselves.

1. Have students sit in a large circle. Each student writes his or her name on a sheet of paper. The student then writes an opening poetic line on the page. (Example: "The snow clings to the giant branches of the protesting palm tree.") Then students pass their papers to the person on their left.

2. The person on the left then adds a line to the poem. (Example: "The palm branch tries to shake the snow onto the frozen ground.") The poem may be free verse or have a rhyme pattern.

   All students should sign their names in the margin next to the new line they wrote. Then they pass the papers again to their left.

3. The next person adds another new line to the poem and signs his or her name in the margin. Then everyone again passes the papers to the left.

4. The process continues as long as the teacher likes, usually until the papers have gone all the way around the circle.

5. Finally the papers are passed back to the original owners. Each person reads the finished poem to the entire class.

ON THEIR FEET

Activities for Speech, Drama, and Special Occasions

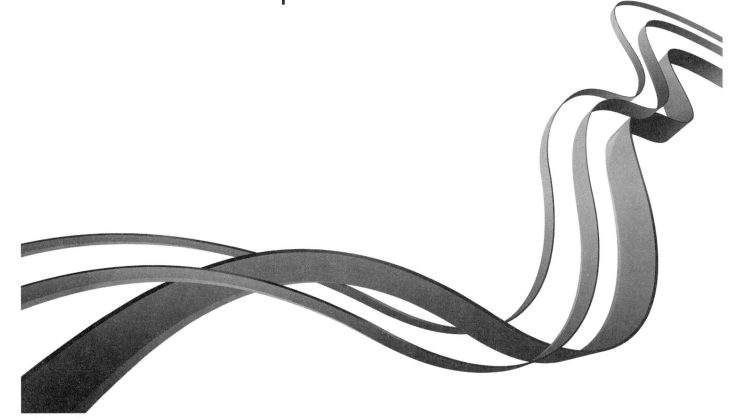

BEWARE OF GREEKS BEARING GIFTS

»THIS ACTIVITY GETS ITS NAME from the legend of the Trojan horse. It sends the message that the outside packaging does not always prepare us for what is inside. The activity works especially well in December or at the end of the year.

1. Have each student bring an object to class wrapped as a gift. The object should just be a "found" object—an empty tube of lipstick, an old ashtray, a paper clip, a hair roller, a plastic toy, a key chain, a marble, etc.

2. Students place their packages into a large box. Be sure that students put their names and class period on the packages they bring, or you may find some inappropriate objects dropped into the box later.

3. Students take turns going to the box, choosing a package, and unwrapping it in front of the class.

4. The person who unwraps an object then has three minutes to make up a story about the object, allowing his or her imagination free rein. For instance, a student might decide that an ashtray is really a swimming pool for ants. The student could then tell the story of the family of ants who lost a family member who drowned in the "pool." The story should last one-three minutes. (To keep things flowing, have one student plan while another student tells his or her story.)

5. A variation of this activity is to have all students unwrap their objects at the same time and then write the stories instead of telling them. Allow students to take turns reading the stories aloud when they are finished.

DICE SPELLING GAME

»THIS GAME HELPS STUDENTS IMPROVE SPELLING SKILLS. You will need two dice and a stopwatch.

1. Divide the class into two teams. One person from the first team goes to the front of the room and rolls the dice. The team member announces the number that appears. Then timing begins. In thirty seconds, the team member must write a word on the board, spelled correctly, with that number of letters. If the person succeeds, that person's team gets a point for each letter in the correctly spelled word. If the person fails, that number is subtracted from the team's total.

2. Then a person from the second team goes to the front of the room and rolls the dice. The team member announces the number and then writes a word on the board with that number of letters. If the word is spelled correctly, that person's team gets points for the number of letters in the correctly spelled word. If the person fails, that number is subtracted from the team's total.

3. The game continues, with one student at a time from alternating teams going to the board. Students may look at their books or other printed material at their desks, but they may not take anything with them to the front of the room. If anyone on a person's team yells out an answer, that person forfeits a turn and the team loses the number of points on the dice.

4. Anyone who rolls a double may use the total from both dice, spelling one word, or total the dice separately, spelling two words. Then the person gets an extra turn (with an additional thirty seconds).

5. When the game becomes too easy, require that the new word begin with the last letter of the previous word. Be sure not to erase the list of words on the board as the game progresses. Words cannot be repeated.

SENIOR PROPHECIES

»THIS ACTIVITY IS A LOT OF FUN if you teach a class that includes some graduating seniors. It is a good way to say good-bye and to help them think about the future.

PROCEDURE

1. Supply a list of senior names to the members of the class.

2. Run off enough copies of the Senior Prophecy handout below so that every class member has a handout for each senior.

3. Give students enough time to complete a Senior Prophecy for each senior.

4. Place a "Prophecy Chair" at the front of the class for the "Senior of Honor." One at a time, the seniors sit in the chair while students read aloud their prophecies for that senior.

5. When the class is finished, the senior stands and reads the prophecy he wrote for himself predicting what he really thinks he will be doing in ten years.

6. Have students pass their prophecies forward for each senior to keep. (Many of my students save their predictions for years. Some even bring them to their class reunions.)

SENIOR PROPHECY   DATE_____

I predict that the following will be true TEN YEARS FROM NOW, about,

_____

1. Your job will be...

2. Your relationship/family status will be ...

3. Your place of residence will be ...

4. Your mode of transportation will be...

5. Something else that will be true about you...

Predictions kindly made by _____

TEAM CHARADES

»CHARADES IS USEFUL in teaching improvisation skills. This version is different from traditional charades because the whole team acts out words for one person who sits in the "guesser's box." It's a kind of backwards charades.

As the teacher, you will need to show the words, keep time, and keep score. You will need a stopwatch and a score pad.

RULES

1. Divide class into teams. Each row can be a team. Teams of four or five students work well. Each team should be differentiated with a name (perhaps Row 1, Row 2, Row 3, etc.).

2. The first team picks a person to be in the guesser's box.

3. Show the rest of the team the first word they will be acting out using pantomime. (No verbal clues are allowed.) As soon as everyone on the team has seen the word, start the stopwatch. All may pantomime individually at the same time, or students may work together. For example, to act out "wedding day," two members might pantomime a bride and groom.

    As soon as the guesser says the word, stop the timer and record one point as the score.

4. Show the team the next word, start the timer again, and repeat the process. The team gets a point for each word guessed in a total of one minute. (If time is called before the last word is guessed, the last word goes to the next team. Therefore, it is very important that no one says the word aloud.)

5. The next team chooses a person for the guesser's box. Show the rest of the team the next word. As soon as everyone on the team has seen it, start timing. Again, team members pantomime clues to the guesser. The team gets a point for each word guessed in one minute.

6. Teams must rotate who goes in the guesser's box. Everyone must have a turn before anyone can repeat.

I have included a word list to use for the game. Of course you may add more words of your own or even supplement with lists that come with other games, such as Pictionary.

(continued)

WORD LIST

eyebrow	skylight	stopwatch	diamond ring	keyboard
hairpiece	black eye	comforter	secret agent	haircut
skyline	trophy	first kiss	commercial	outlaw
toothpaste	overhead projector	tennis shoe	earplug	hairbrush
lipstick	chain saw	bear	payday	alarm clock
curtain rod	bookmark	picture book	window	belt
doorbell	parachute	remote control	scoreboard	free fall
necklace	tightrope	chocolate milk	speed limit	lamp shade
hairnet	trench coat	credit card	mitten	pirate
tee shirt	deer stand	lawn mower	party barge	trampoline
laptop	nail gun	guitar	school bus	wallet
tall tale	ink pen	stoplight	car keys	policeman
bald	countdown	lip ring	knickknack	typewriter
popcorn	recliner	tidal wave	elevator	place mat
helicopter	iguana	dog tags	purse	miracle
earring	sponge	final test	CD player	hubcap
leg warmers	police report	DVD	car chase	dirt road
globe	bad breath	contact lens	nail file	chorus line
snow ski	sports car	monkey	gossip	valentine
hair bow	elephant	sleet	father figure	highway
cough drop	airplane	storm drain	oil can	fast food
tree house	makeup artist	tardy bell	birthday cake	Facebook
news show	headache	prison break	sideburns	bay window
newspaper	shoelace	chalkboard	Tarzan	road trip
sunset	monkey bars	baby bed	flu bug	mailbox

(continued)

TEAM CHARADES

hot air balloon	prison	movie	eyeglasses	time machine
headquarters	fever blister	shipwreck	red carpet	microphone
courtroom	babysitter	picnic table	shopping cart	candy bar
ladder	hero	paper plate	insurance	birthday party
gangster	daydream	bookcase	flag pole	frog prince
station wagon	paper clip	cup hook	eye shadow	parade
bowling ball	Valentine	*American Idol*	bodyguard	electric current
sandbar	dinner party	candlelight	Scotch tape	ocean view
previews	campfire	trailblazer	magic mirror	sewing machine
hillbilly	countdown	Academy Award	Pop-Tarts	tidal wave
holster	doorbell	movie trailer	atomic bomb	bow tie
undercover	helmet	top spot	*The Lion King*	baby blanket
football	crime scene	girlfriend	bubblegum	tablecloth
baby food	salad dressing	true love	tombstone	bridge
split screen	purebred	staircase	sweatshirt	creamed corn
shopping mall	beach	journal	swimming pool	watercolor
sunshine	snack food	cell phone	lifetime	palm reader
mountaintop	handcuffs	tree trunk	fireplace	pizza pan
double dare	x-ray	bathing suit	nose spray	spaceship
steam iron	cable	balance sheet	watermark	guitar player
top secret	ostrich	mountain bike	birdbath	shredded cheese
water boy	family	bug spray	iron skillet	hula hoop
belt loop	coffee can	friendship	car crash	dog food
hiphugger	notepad	cuff link	ruby slippers	time line
weather	squirrel	love song	ants	
armchair	fishing line	microphone	fingerprint	
buttonhole	barbed wire	home run	hair straightener	

PRO-CON GAME

»**PRO-CON GAME HELPS STUDENTS SEE BOTH SIDES** of controversial issues and teaches them to brainstorm and think on their feet. It can be used to introduce persuasive speeches, essays, or debate. You will need a stopwatch or a clock with a second hand.

1. Write topics on slips of paper and put them in a cup. (See below for possible topics.) Ask for volunteers to come forward and draw.

2. The volunteer reads the topic and then begins to speak in favor of the issue (pro side). After thirty seconds, the teacher calls out "Switch!" and the participant immediately switches to the negative side of the issue (con side). The person must completely fill the time—thirty seconds on each side.

POSSIBLE TOPICS

1. Should teenagers be subjected to curfews mandated by the city?

2. Should parents be allowed to censor textbooks and other literature for children in schools?

3. Should cigarettes be illegal?

4. Should newspaper reporters be required to reveal their sources?

5. Should the driving age be raised?

6. Should the government provide child daycare centers for working parents?

7. Should the United States have a mandatory military draft?

8. Should the minimum wage be raised?

9. Should sex education be taught in school?

10. Should organized prayer be permitted in public schools?

11. Have women achieved equality with men in the workplace?

12. Should marriage laws be changed to include same sex partners?

13. Do professional athletes deserve the large salaries they receive?

14. Should schoolteachers have the right to strike?

(continued)

PRO-CON GAME

15. Should schools ban soft drinks and unhealthy snacks?

16. Do blondes really have more fun?

17. Should a school administration have the right to search students' personal possessions?

18. Should schools use metal detectors at school entrances?

19. Should animals be protected from science experiments?

20. Should sex and violence on television or in the movies be restricted?

21. Should all students be required to learn a foreign language in school?

22. Should schools be in session year around?

23. Should schools be allowed to require uniforms?

24. Should movie ratings (G, PG, etc.) be eliminated?

25. Is Hershey's the best chocolate in the world?

26. Is beauty more important than brains?

27. Is reading a lost pastime?

28. Is technology hurting our society?

29. Should teenagers get part-time jobs?

30. Is homeschooling a good idea?

31. Should advertising be banned for children's programming on television?

32. Should students have to pass a test to advance to the next grade?

33. Should teachers be forced to retire at a certain age?

34. Are small schools better than large schools?

35. Which is the best season—winter or spring?

36. Which is worse—being a drug pusher or being a thief?

37. Should seventeen-year-olds be tried in courts as adults?

38. Should retailers say "Happy Holidays" instead of "Merry Christmas?"

39. Should students tell on other students who cheat?

40. Should everyone try to go to college?

TELL ME ABOUT THE TIME...

»THIS ACTIVITY ENCOURAGES STUDENTS to think creatively on their feet and gives them practice with oral communication skills. Print out the scenarios below (or others the class creates) and cut them apart, putting the slips of paper into a container.

Students take turns drawing a scenario and then telling about it, speaking for at least one minute. (Note: The scenarios can also be used as writing prompts.)

TELL ME ABOUT THE TIME...

1.   ...you were hungry and all you could find in the cupboards was Cap'n Crunch.

2.   ...you had to take care of your aunt's triplets.

3.   ...you were swimming across a river and got a leg cramp.

4.   ...you were thrown into a Dumpster.

5.   ...your face got stuck in a yawn.

6.   ...you caught the tooth fairy leaving you only a quarter.

7.   ...your mom drove you and your date to the dance.

8.   ...you borrowed your friend's diamond necklace and lost it.

9.   ...a tornado blew the roof off your house.

10. ...your parents forgot you at the gas station.

11. ...your cat turned into a person.

12. ...you woke up twenty years older.

13. ...a pizza restaurant delivered twenty pizzas to your house.

14. ...your teacher locked all the doors and wouldn't let anyone leave.

15. ...you took a pill and could read people's thoughts.

(continued)

TELL ME ABOUT THE TIME...

16. ...you invented a new food that everyone wanted to buy.

17. ...you came home one hour past your curfew and your dad was waiting for you.

18. ...you wrote a best-selling book that was made into a movie.

19. ...one hundred-dollar bills suddenly rained down on you.

20. ...you locked your keys inside your car.

21. ....you passed into another dimension.

22. ...you flew to the moon.

23. ...you were driving on the freeway and the steering wheel came off in your hands.

24. ...you won a million dollars in the lottery.

25. ...aliens took you in a spaceship to another planet.

26. ...you found a baked potato in your coat pocket.

27. ...you got trapped in a freezer.

28. ...you super-glued your fingers together.

29. ...you bit your dog back.

30. ...you swam the Mississippi River.

31. ...you found a dead rat in your birthday cake.

32. ...your mom came to school with you and attended all your classes.

33. ...a bully took your lunch money.

34. ...you met the ghost who haunts the school.

35. ...you went fishing with your principal.

36....you hit a homerun and won the play-off game.

37. ...you accidentally threw away your retainer at McDonald's.

(continued)

38. ...you were so mad that you punched a locker and broke your hand.

39. ...you escaped an assassin.

40. ...you put salt instead of sugar in your coffee.

41. ...you found a wallet with no identification.

42. ...you lost your little sister in the mall.

43. ...you found a troll living in your basement.

44. ...you dyed your hair and it turned purple.

45. ...you ordered a pizza and didn't have enough money to pay for it.

46. ...you fell off the stage during a play.

47. ....you accidentally washed your cat in the dishwasher.

48. ...you found a magic lamp.

49. ...Simon Cowell knocked on your door and begged you to be on *American Idol*.

50. ...you forgot to brush your teeth.

51. ...your nose fell off your face.

52. ...your cell phone rang during class.

53. ...you got switches and ashes for Christmas.

54. ...no one came to your birthday party.

55. ...you sailed the ocean with pirates.

56. ...you were in a shoot-out with a cowboy.

57. ...you discovered that your parents were aliens.

58. ...you stopped a bullet with your hand.

59. ...you ordered a new family.

60. ...you were on *Oprah*.

WHAT'S IN THE BOX?

»PANTOMIME IS THE ART OF TELLING A STORY using body movements and gestures to communicate with the audience. "What's in the Box?" teaches pantomime techniques and helps students learn to read body language and improve acting skills. It is also useful in speech classes to teach students how to use their bodies effectively when speaking.

1. A student volunteers (or is chosen) to be the "actor." The actor thinks of something that would fit inside a box. It doesn't have to necessarily come in a box; it just needs to be able to fit into one.

2. The actor begins by announcing "Ready!" to the class. This is like raising the curtain. At this point, there should be no talking in the class.

3. Using gestures, the person defines the size of the box. The box might be very small or very large.

4. Next the person pantomimes opening the box and taking the object out.

5. Then the person should do something to show what the object is—drink out of a cup, put on a contact lens, use a tennis racket, dig a hole with a shovel, etc. He or she can use no actual props. The props are suggested by gestures.

6. The person ends by announcing "Finished!" to the class. This is like lowering the curtain. At that point, class members may raise their hands and, when called on, guess what object is in the box.

This activity can also be used to introduce Thorton Wilder's play *Our Town*. This play uses very little scenery and props. Almost everything the actors do is pantomimed. For example, Emily and George sit in front of a board stretched across the backs of two chairs to simulate a soda fountain. They profess their love for each other as they pantomime drinking floats through straws. In another scene, the two families come down to the breakfast table and pantomime eating and reading the paper. Students readily act out scenes from the play after playing "What's in the Box?"

PICTURES ALIVE!

»"PICTURES ALIVE!" HELPS STUDENTS learn about methods of indirect characterization. You will need a magazine picture of a person for each member in your class. Don't use any famous people. Try to get a diverse group of people—different ages, occupations, races, degrees of beauty, etc.

INDIRECT CHARACTERIZATION

The audience/reader makes judgments about a character's personality based on the following:

1. The character's appearance
2. The character's speech
3. The character's actions
4. What other characters say about the character

PROCEDURE

1. Give all students a picture, and ask them not to let anyone else see their picture. Have class members spread out in the room, study their pictures, and prepare to "become" the person in the picture. Each student should decide what kind of life the person in the picture leads, how old the person is, how the person would talk, how the person would carry himself/herself, how the character would dress, what kind of attitudes this person would have, etc. After about five minutes, collect the pictures.

2. Explain that when you announce "time," students are to "transform" into the person in their picture. The characters will all be at a party that will last for about ten minutes. During this time they are to talk to everyone present, in character, and try to learn as much as they can about each other.

3. At the end of the party, show each picture one at a time and ask class members to guess who played the person in that picture. Students will actively be using the indirect characterization methods listed above to make their determinations.

4. As a follow-up, you may want to have students write a short memoir written in the voice of the character they became.

ALPHABET DIALOGUE

»ALPHABET DIALOGUE USES IMPROVISATION to give students practice with the valuable skill of thinking on their feet. To be successful, each student must focus on what the other student is saying and then create a new line. Students learn valuable listening skills, exercise creative thinking, and develop teamwork skills.

Three people at a time play the game in front of the class.

1. The first person (A) begins the dialogue using a word that begins with any letter of the alphabet.

2. The second person (B) must begin the next line using a word that begins with the next letter of the alphabet.

3. Then (A) begins the next line using a word that begins with the next letter; then (B) begins the next line using a word that begins with the next letter, and so on.

4. At any point, the third person (C) may interrupt and say a line starting with a word that begins with any letter. This allows (A) to change the pattern and begin a new line with any letter of the alphabet.

EXAMPLE

A: **L**ife is like a box of chocolates.

B: **M**iss, why are you talking to me?

A: **N**ever make fun of me. My mama says...

B: **O**h, I don't care what your mama says.

A: **P**apa then? Do you care what he says?

C: **H**ey, do y'all have any money?

A: **G**et a job, you slob!

B: **H**old on! You can't talk like that!

A: **I** can do whatever I want!

C: **D**o you have any money?

A: **A**lways I say, get a job!

B: **B**ack off, crazy person! I'm going home!

A: **C**ome back! Teach me Japanese!

C: **A**ll I need is a dollar.

A: **G**et it from the Japanese man over here!

B: **H**ey! I'm not Japanese!

A: **I** am! I love Japan! Go Japan!

C: **Y**eah, but Japan doesn't have American money.

A: **B**ut they do have yen.

B: **C**an you please stop talking?!

A: **D**on't yell! I'm sorry. I will stop.

C: **W**ait! Come back and give me a dollar!

If this activity seems too difficult at first, try doing it as a written activity and then let each group read its dialogue for the class.

ALPHABET SENTENCE

A variation of this exercise is a written one. Students write one sentence, each word starting with a successive letter of the alphabet. Punctuation is allowed, but not periods. I use this activity as a challenge at the end of a class.

The resulting sentences may not make a lot of sense, but it's an interesting and difficult challenge for students. Here's an example:

All brilliant creatures dutifully entice funny green hippos into juggling kittenish lemmings, mostly near old public quaint restaurants, tempting us violently with x-rayed yellow zippers.

If the exercise is too difficult, a variation is to allow multiple sentences instead of only one.

REACTING TO A PROP

»STUDENTS USE BODY LANGUAGE to react to various props in this exercise. It helps them refine communication skills and gives them practice in exercising creativity.

PROCEDURE

Arrange students in a circle. Explain that they are to imagine that the objects you will pass around are *not* what they seem. Students are to imagine that the objects have become different items that you suggest, and they should react and handle the objects as though the objects really have transformed into whatever they have been told. Each time an object is passed on, the suggested idea changes.

POSSIBLE OBJECTS

- Stuffed animal: Pretend it is a newborn baby, a kitten, a bag of flour, a baby porcupine, a hot potato, a human heart, a baby alligator, etc.

- A book: Pretend it is a "little black book," a cookbook, a photo album, a baby book, an atlas, a container of explosive material, a box of candy, a jewelry box, etc.

- A rock: Pretend it is a diamond, a bullet, a cockroach, a piece of chocolate, a silver dollar, a magic pill, a flower, etc.

- People's choice: Choose an item and ask each student to decide what it is. An ink pen might become a nail file, a nail, a screwdriver, a chisel, a thermometer, a cigarette, a knife, a gun, a can-opener, a key, etc. This time the item changes with each person.

PAIR IMPROVISATIONS

»WITH IMPROVISATION, STUDENTS ACT OUT SCENES with little or no preparation. They must observe each other's body language, really listen to what another person is saying in order to create the next line, and work together to create a believable scene. Improvisation develops observation skills, listening skills, and teamwork.

Each of the scenarios below can be used for improvisations. The students take their positions at the front of the room "on stage." When they are ready, one says, "Ready" to simulate the raising of the curtain. From that moment on, class members should cease talking. Class members are not allowed to offer ideas or help the performers in any way. They may laugh at appropriate times only. When the performers are through, one says, "Finished" to simulate the curtain going down. At this point class members may clap. Each improvisation should last one to three minutes.

SCENARIOS

1. A teenager is coming home one hour past curfew. When the teen enters, the angry mother is waiting.

2. A salesperson comes to a homeowner's door and is determined not to leave until the homeowner has bought a vacuum cleaner.

3. A hypochondriac is trying to convince a doctor to prescribe pills for his or her imaginary illness.

4. A teacher is writing on the chalkboard. Suddenly, a student throws a paper wad and hits the teacher on the back.

5. A supervisor must fire a person who desperately needs the income.

6. A very poor man is trying to get a loan to start a business at the bank. The banker treats him with contempt.

7. A small child is lost in a crowd. A passerby stops to help.

8. A teenager has just failed his driving test and must tell his best friend.

9. An irate neighbor comes to complain to a teenager that the teen's music is too loud.

(continued)

PAIR IMPROVISATIONS

10. The telephone rings and an elderly woman answers it. The caller is an escaped convict.

11. A teenager has just been fired from his job for stealing and must tell the parent.

12. A man is attending his ten-year class reunion. He meets the girl he was secretly in love with all through high school.

13. Two teens on a date are watching a movie in a crowded theater. Someone yells, "Fire!"

14. An engaged couple argues about whether or not one of them should get a tattoo.

15. Two people are trapped in an elevator. One of them is claustrophobic.

16. A teenage boy is picking up his date for the first time and the girl isn't ready. He must spend a long time talking to her father.

17. Two friends are at an awards banquet. Both are nominated for an award. Only one wins. The other comes in last.

18. A police officer has to explain to parents why their son or daughter has been arrested.

19. One friend tries to convince another friend that she has a talking dog.

20. At a party, a woman runs into the ex-boss who fired her.

21. A neighbor's dog has gotten loose and has injured the homeowner's cat.

22. A little girl lets a kitten follow her home. She tries to convince her father to let her keep the cat.

23. A football player who has just lost the big game for his team enters the locker room to talk to his best friend.

24. Two young children approach what they think is a haunted house. One wants to go in but the other is too frightened.

25. Two people are playing with a Ouija board. One tries to convince the other that the game has supernatural powers.

26. A mother and daughter are shopping for a prom dress. The mother wants the girl to dress conservatively, but the girl thinks the mom is old-fashioned.

27. A little boy tries to convince his parents to raise his allowance.

28. A movie star meets an admiring fan.

(continued)

29. A little boy is very afraid of shots and crawls under a table at the doctor's office. A parent is trying to get him out.

30. A person in a movie theater is quite annoyed by someone in front of him who will not stop talking.

31. A young woman runs out of gas on the side of the road. A stranger stops to offer help.

32. A singer comes onstage to receive an award, presented by another musician, for best new song.

33. One student on his way back to class sees another student pull the fire alarm for no reason.

34. Two friends are shopping in a department store. One sees the other shoplift something.

35. An engaged couple is trapped at the top of a Ferris wheel. One is terrified; the other is excited, leading to a major disagreement.

36. A student in a class sees another person copying off his paper without permission.

37. A bank robber is trying to steal from a teller who is hard of hearing.

38. A person's best friend re-gifts the present the friend gave him or her last year.

39. A little girl is terrified by the monster in her closet. The babysitter is trying to get the little girl to fall asleep.

40. A boy catches his girlfriend in a lie.

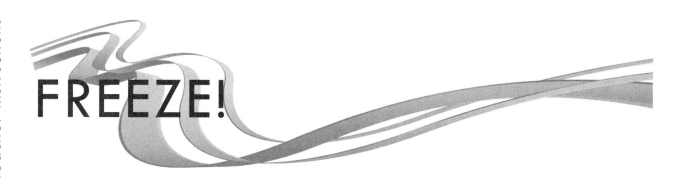

FREEZE!

»TO PRACTICE VERBAL AND BODY LANGUAGE communication skills, start with two people "on stage." They will begin an improvisation. Let the improvisation develop for at least thirty seconds. After that point, any member of the class may yell, "Freeze!"

That person then goes to the front of the room and takes the place of one of the people in the improvisation. The new person should assume the exact position of the person whose place is being taken. The new person says, "Action!" and the skit continues.

Each person in the class should take someone's place at some point during the game. With the addition of each new person, the skit can change. The person who remains should change to fit in with what the new person is doing.

PUPPET MASTER AND PUPPET

»THIS IS AN IMPROVISATION GAME that focuses on communicating with body language and developing creativity. Students learn to react to each other's body language and then create the dialogue to go with that reaction.

The game involves two couples "on stage." One person in each pair is the puppet; the other is the puppet master. It is best if girls are paired with girls and boys are paired with boys.

The puppet master in each pair positions his or her puppet in a pose, being careful not to touch the puppet inappropriately or pose the puppet in an inappropriate position. The two puppets must then look at each other and decide some logical reason for being in their poses. One of the puppet masters calls, "Action!" and the puppets begin to move and speak.

The puppet masters control the puppets throughout the scene. The puppets must make their actions and words go together. They must stay in their basic poses but may add movement appropriate to that pose until moved into a new basic pose by their puppet masters.

For example, a puppet master might pose his puppet with an arm raised and the index finger of the raised hand touching the puppet's teeth. The puppet decides that he is brushing his teeth. He may move his finger up and down, but he cannot lower his arm until the puppet master re-poses him. Or a puppet may have one leg raised. He may decide that he is running in place and move both legs appropriately until his puppet master repositions him into a seated position.

MAGIC MERRY-GO-ROUND OF DANGER

»MAGIC MERRY-GO-ROUND OF DANGER is an improvisation game that focuses on developing creativity skills. Students create scenes of danger and communicate the scenes to the class through body language and dialogue.

Two students take their position "on stage" at the front of the class. They lock arms and twirl in a circle several times to simulate a magic merry-go-round that will transport the pair to another place or time. The merry-go-round drops its passengers only at times and places of danger. When the teacher directs the merry-go-round to stop, the two must get off and begin their improvisation.

Pairs may decide beforehand what the situations will be, but the actions and dialogue are improvisations. The two students must decide whether they are in the past or future and what danger they are in. They must survive until they can get back on the merry-go-round. But each time the merry-go-round stops, they enter a new place and must confront a new danger.

LISTS, LISTS, LISTS

For Freewrites, Skits, Composition, Improvisation, Speech, and Playing with Language

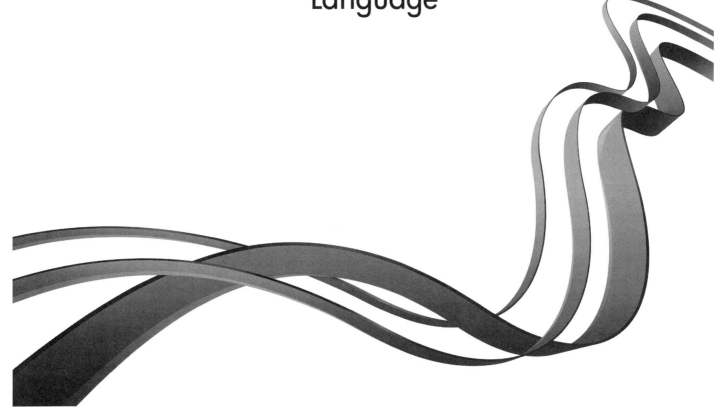

USING LISTS, LISTS, LISTS

»THIS SECTION IS MADE UP OF, YES, LISTS. It includes a list of opening lines of dialogue, a list of poetic starters, a list of items, a list of places, a list of characters, a list of proverbs, and a list of situations.

What do you do with the lists? Here are some ideas:

- Use any of the lists as an excellent source for freewrite topics. A freewrite is a timed writing assignment in which students are asked to write for a period of time (usually five to ten minutes) without stopping. They may write a story, a poem, a rant, a description, a dialogue, a play, or whatever else they want. The idea is to get them to write freely.

  Students must write for the entire time. If they run out of ideas in one area, they may stop and start another idea. They should not be concerned about punctuation, spelling, or grammar, although it is certainly acceptable to write correctly. The work is usually graded for completion, not correctness.

  After students write, they may read their writing aloud to the class. (They may pass on reading aloud only if the writing is personal.) This activity gives students a strong sense of audience.

- Use the lists separately or in combination. For example, you might ask students to write a story or do an improvisation that combines a certain item number from several lists. Item #14 from the first five lists that follow would include *"I was in a hurry," "Narcolepsy makes class bearable,"* hammer, the pier, and teenager.

- Use "Opening Lines" for class skits or improvisations. The students performing the improvisations decide where they are, who is involved, what the conflict is, etc., and then begin.

  "Opening Lines" can also be used for exercises in writing dialogue.

- Use "Poetic Starters" for poems or short stories.

- Use the "Items" list to play "UPS Driver." A student pantomimes the following: The doorbell rings, but he or she finds no one at the door. However, there is a package. The student opens the package and discovers one of the items on the list. The class tries to guess the item, based on the student's pantomime.

  Another use is to ask students to personify items from the list, or to write similes or metaphors using items from the list.

(continued)

USING LISTS, LISTS, LISTS

» continued

- Have students write "Where I Went on My Summer Vacation" stories, using the "Places" list. Students write about a supposed visit to one of the places, making the visit sound believable and enticing to others.

  Students can also write scene descriptions using the "Places" list.

- Play "Elevator Talk" with the "Characters" list. Two random characters from the list meet in the elevator and carry on a conversation. Students may write out a dialogue, or the activity may be used as an improvisation.

  Another use is to play "Fix It." Put two characters from the list together and give them a problem they must solve. (They are stuck in an elevator; one of them has a flat tire; they are involved in a national security issue, etc.)

  Another improvisation to try is "Guess Who's Coming to Dinner." A family welcomes a character (or characters) to dinner. The character knows who he or she is, but the family doesn't. The family (and the class members) must figure out who the guest is through actions and dialogue.

- Assign items from the "Proverbs" list and ask students to write a story or perform a skit that proves the truth of the proverb.

  The "Proverbs" list also works well for playing Charades.

- The "Prompts" list is perfect for essays, debates, improvisations, and story starters. Some are fairly specific, but many are purposely vague.

  Oftentimes, we teachers give our students too much structure in writing prompts, and students aren't interested or feel stifled. My students prefer vague topics and are much more creative in responding to them.

  There are countless other ways to use the various lists. You and your students are limited only by your own imaginations.

OPENING LINES

1. Are you going to eat that?
2. What did you do with the directions?
3. My name is not Peter.
4. What's that on your back?
5. Which way did he go?
6. Have we met?
7. I think they forgot about the party.
8. I've got a bad feeling about this.
9. Not that one! This one!
10. I hate this show.
11. You said you were going to change.
12. I really shouldn't tell anyone, but...
13. I know there's money in there.
14. I was in a hurry.
15. He clearly hadn't taken a shower in a long time.
16. I think it's coming from the basement.
17. Has anybody seen Stanley?
18. Why don't you say that to my face?
19. Let's step outside.
20. It's coming from inside the house.
21. You stole my shirt!
22. This town's not big enough for both of us.
23. Are we there yet?
24. You should have told me.
25. I thought you were leaving.
26. It's nothing serious, but...

27. It's not my fault.
28. It's almost over.
29. He didn't say good-bye.
30. That wasn't part of the deal.
31. Is that lipstick on your collar?
32. It seemed like a good idea.
33. I just want to be friends.
34. I refuse to star in your psychodrama.
35. I'll be back.
36. Are we lost?
37. Could you tell me how to get to ___?
38. I wouldn't drink that if I were you.
39. Surely you can't be serious.
40. There was water, water everywhere.
41. I don't like it.
42. Cut the blue wire.
43. My name is not Gladys.
44. Does anybody here know how to fly a plane?
45. Is there a doctor in the house?
46. Was this trip really necessary?
47. You remind me of myself at your age.
48. Does anybody here know CPR?
49. It starts at eight.
50. I'll take it back.
51. I feel like I am going to faint.
52. That's not where I left it.
53. Did you hear that?

(continued)

54. Stay here.

55. Whatever made you think that was a good idea?

56. What a wonderful smell you have discovered.

57. Where did you hide it?

58. Can you drive a standard?

59. I think we just ran over something.

60. It was on fire when I got here.

61. How much do you want for that thing?

62. How long do we have to stay here?

63. Whoa! Put the knife away!

64. What is your location?

65. Did she really say that?

66. We have a winner!

67. I see you're drinking skim milk.

68. What's that noise?

69. I didn't do nothin.'

70. I want my lawyer.

71. Where were you on the night of ___?

72. Have I got a deal for you!

73. Where should I put these?

74. Do you speak English?

75. Does it hurt?

76. I don't think this is a cave.

77. Well, my dad...

78. Did you do your homework?

79. I read it in a book.

80. What are the chances that this could happen?

81. It's nice to finally put a face with a name.

82. Make my day.

83. I think you've got it upside down.

84. So, we meet again.

85. The oxygen masks will fall shortly.

86. It's merely a flesh wound.

87. I've gotta go.

88. Do you want fries with that?

89. Do you feel lucky?

90. I'm not dead.

91. I just hate when that happens.

92. Stop! I mean it!

93. Put your hands above your head!

94. My mamma always told me...

95. I forgot.

96. Pain, darkness, the sound of a scream...

97. He should have been here an hour ago.

98. Does anyone else think this is a little weird?

99. Don't worry; be happy.

100. Let's just pretend like this never happened.

101. Am I allowed to talk?

102. Look at me in the face.

103. Don't interrupt me.

104. What's in my chili?

105. There was something strange about that guy.

106. Does the wall feel warm to you?

107. Is your mother home?

108. Don't open the door!

109. Not now!

110. How many times do I have to tell you?

(continued)

111. Can you help me find my dog?

112. Release the hounds!

113. How many hostages does he have?

114. Is something burning?

115. How long before the rest of them hatch?

116. Did you say snakes? On a plane?

117. It's alive!

118. Where did you hide the money?

119. It's the police!

120. Sir, I would like to ask for your daughter's hand in marriage.

121. Take cover.

122. It's ticking.

123. I'm from the future.

124. Honey, the sheriff's here to see you.

125. It just never ends, does it?

126. You hold it while I hit it.

127. Silver bullets only work in the movies.

128. I told you never to trust a clown.

129. You can't get them wet.

130. I am not going to be responsible for that.

131. Have you found her?

132. You should have unplugged it first.

133. How old is this?

134. I think we blew a fuse.

135. Et tu, Brute?

136. Are we going the right way?

137. You're going too fast.

138. Honey, just stop and ask directions.

139. Be very quiet. Don't move.

140. Do you mind?

141. Is this seat taken?

142. Which tie should I wear?

143. You cut it out wrong.

144. My hero!

145. Did he beat you?

146. This is magic.

147. You just can't keep anything nice around here.

148. Call 9-1-1.

149. That's neither here nor there. It's in the past.

150. It was Greek to me.

151. Everyone feels guilty, but no one is at fault.

152. I can't stop crying.

153. If I throw a stick, will you leave?

154. Are you sure?

155. I can't get it open.

156. Would you like to dance?

157. Boys will be boys.

158. Some of those teachers need to go back to school.

159. Is she breathing?

160. You know, I had the strangest dream...

161. Where have you been?

162. Why are you late?

163. Stop talking!

164. I don't believe you.

165. Can't we all just get along?

(continued)

OPENING LINES

166. You've put up a wall.

167. Why do you insist on _____?

168. We are not alone.

169. You will never believe this!

170. I want to scream.

171. When will you know?

172. This must be a dream.

173. The ambulance is on the way.

174. That was last week.

175. Is it Friday yet?

176. Put the gun away.

177. This is being recorded.

178. You missed!

179. How did you vote?

180. This is the best day of my life!

181. What are you saying?

182. Paper or plastic?

183. How are you feeling?

184. Life's not fair.

185. What time is this over?

186. What is the last thing you remember?

187. You're getting sleepy.

188. I can't find my marbles.

189. It's fragile.

190. I'm learning.

191. Was that a red light?

192. The flowers are poison.

193. Is it contagious?

194. I warned you I couldn't cook.

195. What's behind door number two?

196. I've been struck by lightning.

197. We're moving again.

198. Your words are nonsense.

199. I think the elevator's stuck.

200. Was I speeding?

201. He ate my ring.

202. I live in a glass house.

203. I can't see.

204. What exactly are you saying?

205. Which end goes up?

206. I was watching that.

207. Have you seen the remote?

208. And who is this?

209. Your chariot awaits.

210. Where's the bride?

211. Clean up in aisle four.

212. Have you seen the remote?

213. You're five dollars short.

214. There's a policeman at the door.

215. My dog ate it.

216. Do you have cotton in your ears?

217. Ask her the due date.

218. She's just a girl.

219. He's just a boy.

220. I think we're in trouble now.

221. None of my friends has a curfew.

POETIC STARTERS

1. I'm walking on a tightrope.

2. I exhale toxic fumes of black smoke.

3. His intentions shatter on the tile floor.

4. My white horse ran off with my prince.

5. Write me a love song.

6. You're the reason I lose sleep at night.

7. Time marks our calendars.

8. Faces are tattooed in my mind.

9. These are hard words to swallow.

10. My wings fell off.

11. I have become the status quo.

12. Her tears fell like sweat from sad eyes.

13. My life's fabric is unraveling.

14. Narcolepsy makes class bearable.

15. She molded me like paraffin.

16. A big black horse bade me follow.

17. Pieces of you surround me.

18. My life is a treadmill.

19. Plastic people smile.

20. Time is a plastic bubble.

21. Every person's blood is red like mine.

22. He used to bring me flowers.

23. A malevolent whisper comes from within.

24. The chocolate pudding pushed me across the floor.

25. She leads a double life.

26. The dream lady visits me.

27. My kite is caught in your tree.

28. I feel alone in a crowd.

29. You give my heart hunger pains.

30. He haunts my dreams.

31. My melody bled out.

32. Where can I hide when I can't disappear?

33. My paper-thin dream dies.

34. How do I rewind this scene of my life?

35. Conformity is our friend.

36. Shortly I will burst into flames.

37. I get baptized in your love.

38. I have a circus in my head.

39. You whisper words that melt.

40. The colors of my picture spin onto the floor.

41. Drops of rain trail down the pane.

42. The little red wagon lay crushed in the street.

43. He's my drug of choice.

44. Fast cars whiz in the slow rain.

45. He causes flowers to wilt.

46. He's no superman.

47. The portrait fades before my eyes.

(continued)

48. Believe in the lie.

49. The last sands of his hourglass fall.

50. I drown in the sound of my own screaming.

51. The wind whispers to me.

52. The raindrops tell a story.

53. Silence can be violent.

54. Erase the tablet of my mind.

55. I'm haunted by your silhouette.

56. Her eyes were full of empty.

57. It devours your shadow.

58. Our love is stripped and polished.

59. I have my own parasite.

60. You make my walls crumble.

61. His words fly into my heart.

62. I'm on the other side of a fun house mirror.

63. I dream on a silver screen.

64. Destruction breeds creation.

65. We create a new constellation.

66. Your voice is the soundtrack of my dreams.

67. I'm walking on a tightrope.

68. The words wrap me in vines.

69. We speak in silent voices.

70. Fireflies open a light show.

71. I paint my poems in desert sand.

72. It's the edge of the world.

73. My prince lost his crown.

74. Rain fills spaces with humid silence.

75. His carved, wooden face never moved.

76. He left me napkins to write verses on.

77. When I was in love, she wasn't.

78. See what you will in the flames.

79. Wet footprints in the sand dissolve.

80. Children sway and dip to the rhythm of life.

81. She becomes a beautiful swan.

82. Like a phoenix, I rise again.

83. We are cookie-cutter people.

84. You are my compass and my chart.

85. My mirror lies.

86. I go back to nowhere from where I came.

87. I skate on thin ice.

88. I pay a debt to loneliness.

89. We are tattered gypsies seeking friendly faces.

90. I've got a room full of feathers.

91. I put your hair in a jar.

92. My eyes long to kiss your face.

93. He talks in symbols.

94. In my dreams there are eyes like yours.

95. She dances pretty to his tune.

96. The river wraps its cold arms around me.

97. The line I wrote is a lie.

98. Dreams leave no fingerprints.

99. I'm grapes fermented.

100. I'm haunted by your silhouette.

ITEMS

1. keys
2. artificial flowers
3. diamond necklace
4. credit card
5. mousetrap
6. screwdriver
7. water bottle
8. ancient book
9. telescope
10. whoopee cushion
11. calculator
12. map
13. locked box
14. hammer
15. binoculars
16. unpublished manuscript
17. "Baby on Board" sign
18. senior ring
19. pick-up truck
20. x-ray machine
21. trap door
22. wallet
23. 3-D glasses
24. pirate ship
25. Bunsen burner
26. jewelry box
27. Samurai sword
28. duct tape
29. sticker
30. Porsche
31. nail file
32. snow
33. frying pan
34. bongo drum
35. shrunken head
36. stick of gum
37. book
38. grade book
39. broom
40. wig
41. gavel
42. envelope
43. ankle weights
44. plane ticket
45. chest of drawers
46. music CD
47. deck of cards
48. glasses
49. keyboard
50. popcorn
51. watch
52. rain
53. bookshelf
54. teepee
55. Jell-O
56. road sign
57. sleet
58. banjo
59. hurricane
60. skull
61. rope
62. candlestick
63. fork
64. iPod
65. cat
66. diaper
67. bird
68. urn
69. missile
70. hammock
71. cork
72. baked potato
73. airplane
74. dog
75. transporter
76. shotgun
77. cat food
78. uniform
79. sushi
80. ray gun
81. a ring
82. pyramid
83. lemon
84. roaches

(continued)

ITEMS

85. fish	116. icicle	147. paint can
86. cow	117. calf	148. basket
87. Christmas tree	118. steer	149. mirror
88. wire coat hanger	119. wagon train	150. rabbit's foot
89. time machine	120. pothole	151. earring
90. avalanche	121. pond	152. wedding band
91. Twinkies	122. dust mite	153. contact lens
92. speeding ticket	123. egg	154. baseball bat
93. hair dye	124. sunflower	155. Ferris wheel
94. subpoena	125. ski lift	156. ambulance
95. tapestry	126. volcano	157. perfume
96. slingshot	127. bow and arrow	158. rocking chair
97. cornmeal	128. feather	159. receipt
98. siren	129. orange	160. Tupperware
99. sheet music	130. cowboy hat	161. notebook
100. present	131. beaded hat	162. paper doll
101. sunglasses	132. helmet	163. backbone
102. rocket	133. motorcycle	164. poison ivy
103. poison dart	134. Mardi Gras beads	165. chalkboard
104. saddle	135. doubloon	166. window
105. flat tire	136. plastic cup	167. applesauce
106. suit of armor	137. crown	168. coffee
107. campfire	138. pieces of gold	169. hot dogs
108. stagecoach	139. compass	170. cardboard box
109. pizza	140. umbrella	171. pacifier
110. hollow tree	141. tweezers	172. blanket
111. squeaky gate	142. crayons	173. football
112. deserted road	143. flamingo	174. iPhone
113. mask	144. pen	175. remote control
114. chain saw	145. purse	
115. souvenir	146. Christmas lights	

PLACES

1. rose garden
2. church auditorium
3. coffee shop
4. amusement park
5. football stadium
6. rock concert
7. dark alley
8. Hawaiian luau
9. mountaintop
10. flea market
11. jail cell
12. department store
13. beauty salon
14. the pier
15. on the farm
16. pawnshop
17. ski boat
18. train station
19. desert oasis
20. swimming pool
21. bank
22. golf course
23. wedding reception
24. boat in shark infested waters
25. submarine
26. spaceship
27. warehouse

28. shoe store
29. truck stop
30. movie theater
31. coal mine
32. subway station
33. country road
34. mansion
35. houseboat
36. museum
37. kitchen
38. terrorist training camp
39. White House
40. forest
41. college dorm room
42. cruise ship
43. ballroom
44. classroom
45. beach
46. mud hut
47. tower
48. castle
49. ancient ruins
50. daycare center
51. grocery store
52. dining room
53. garage
54. elevator
55. hospital waiting room

56. ski resort
57. a preschool
58. corral
59. slaughterhouse
60. plantation
61. deserted house
62. circus
63. zoo
64. log cabin
65. the market
66. anti-war protest rally
67. swamp
68. bus station
69. flood area
70. phone booth
71. ballpark
72. parking lot
73. street corner
74. hostel
75. sewers
76. parade route
77. dollar store
78. opera house
79. graveyard
80. funeral home
81. class reunion
82. storeroom

(continued)

PLACES

83. closet
84. amphitheater
85. locker room
86. library
87. sunroom
88. front porch
89. barn
90. toy store
91. lighthouse
92. courtroom
93. Department of Motor Vehicles
94. school dance
95. family Thanksgiving
96. rainforest
97. pulpit
98. dentist office
99. barbershop
100. paintball arena
101. checkout line
102. corn maze
103. jury room
104. skating rink
105. airplane cabin
106. stairwell
107. summer camp
108. patio
109. bus stop
110. chartered bus
111. bush taxi

112. principal's office
113. construction site
114. tunnel
115. bridal shower
116. train
117. taxi
118. cabin
119. sitting room
120. tent
121. dry cleaner
122. bakery
123. research lab
124. shrimp boat
125. Shakespeare festival
126. gym
127. fitness center
128. ballet studio
129. beauty salon
130. treehouse
131. emergency room
132. operating room
133. pet shop
134. restaurant
135. lookout point
136. jewelry store
137. church nursery
138. cathedral
139. busy street corner
140. supermarket
141. space station

142. space shuttle
143. lion's cage
144. cyberspace
145. capital building
146. haunted house
147. forensics lab
148. workshop
149. baby boutique
150. pet groomer
151. moon
152. hot air balloon
153. used car lot
154. rooftop
155. auction
156. bowling alley
157. paradise
158. greenhouse
159. storm shelter
160. dungeon
161. harbor
162. garden
163. trash can
164. bazaar
165. wharf
166. eye of a hurricane
167. soup kitchen
168. cellar
169. cloud nine
170. snow cone stand

CHARACTERS

1. doctor
2. cheerleader
3. policeman
4. drug dealer
5. blonde
6. nurse
7. nerd
8. geek
9. Goth
10. tour guide
11. controlling mother
12. grocery bagger
13. grandparent
14. teenager
15. jock
16. mad scientist
17. mama's boy
18. obsessed fan
19. a new mother
20. sergeant
21. thief
22. alien
23. pilot
24. teacher
25. alcoholic

26. drug addict
27. artist
28. ex-wife
29. stepmother
30. bullfighter
31. banker
32. soldier
33. professor
34. construction worker
35. Kung Fu master
36. convict on death row
37. substitute teacher
38. delivery person
39. nanny
40. Wal-Mart greeter
41. ninety-three-year-old woman
42. ninety-three-year-old man
43. cashier
44. two year old
45. truck driver
46. waiter
47. waitress

48. maitre d'
49. bully
50. princess
51. beauty queen
52. musician
53. pirate
54. poet
55. ditz
56. Peace Corps volunteer
57. village chief
58. choir director
59. southern belle
60. politician
61. governor
62. monk
63. priest
64. exterminator
65. street performer
66. dancer
67. singer
68. plumber
69. janitor
70. hitchhiker
71. genius
72. child prodigy

73. taxi driver
74. gambler
75. cowboy
76. frat boy
77. night watchman
78. hit man
79. mobster
80. cat burglar
81. backwoodsman
82. fisherman
83. big game hunter
84. newborn
85. knight
86. lawyer
87. treasure hunter
88. little boy/girl
89. con artist
90. dentist
91. circus performer
92. talk show host
93. weather forecaster
94. news anchor
95. bartender
96. blacksmith
97. vampire

CHARACTERS

98. door-to-door salesperson
99. car salesperson
100. peddler
101. town crier
102. superhero
103. bum
104. homeless person
105. lumberjack
106. shop owner
107. executioner
108. beekeeper
109. watchmaker
110. carpenter
111. seamstress
112. Ninja
113. jester
114. king/queen
115. actor/actress
116. therapist
117. farmer
118. thief
119. secret agent
120. chauffeur
121. gravely ill person
122. disabled person
123. shepherd

124. skater
125. dancer
126. conjoined twins
127. gnome
128. fairy god-mother
129. nun
130. trapeze artist
131. writer
132. baker
133. rap star
134. hippie
135. protester
136. astronaut
137. robot
138. terrorist
139. milkman
140. paper boy
141. orphan
142. rocket scientist
143. barbarian
144. Viking
145. marathon runner
146. graduate
147. cat lady
148. heavy equipment operator
149. inventor

150. baby
151. lifeguard
152. surfer
153. preacher
154. model
155. philanthropist
156. billionaire
157. sailor
158. computer programmer
159. engineer
160. umpire
161. miner
162. tap dancer
163. caddy
164. band leader
165. principal
166. tyrant
167. chemist
168. godfather
169. hostage
170. singer
171. babysitter
172. ballerina
173. carnival barker
174. pharmacist
175. bus driver
176. lottery winner
177. mailman

178. housekeeper
179. tattoo artist
180. wrestler
181. fortune-teller
182. dog walker
183. referee
184. proctor
185. nominee
186. deputy
187. volunteer
188. marathon runner
189. servant
190. guardian
191. photographer
192. pest
193. jester
194. comedian
195. mime
196. bandit
197. swindler
198. secret agent
199. hip-hop artist
200. hairstylist

PROVERBS

1. The shortest distance between two points is a straight line.

2. A penny saved is a penny earned.

3. Absence makes the heart grow fonder.

4. When the cat's away, the mice will play.

5. Actions speak louder than words.

6. All work and no play makes Jack a dull boy.

7. It's the little things in life that count.

8. Good things come to those who wait.

9. A stitch in time saves nine.

10. All's fair in love and war.

11. A bird in the hand is worth two in the bush.

12. Curiosity killed the cat.

13. A fool and his money are soon parted.

14. An apple a day keeps the doctor away.

15. A rolling stone gathers no moss.

16. A friend in need is a friend indeed.

17. Ask and you shall receive.

18. A man is known by the company he keeps.

19. No pain, no gain.

20. Old habits die hard.

21. Don't judge a book by its cover.

22. All that glitters is not gold.

23. Don't count your chickens before they hatch.

24. A little knowledge is a dangerous thing.

25. A picture is worth a thousand words.

26. All's well that ends well.

27. Garbage in, garbage out.

28. People who live in glass houses shouldn't throw stones.

29. Don't cry over spilt milk.

30. Haste makes waste.

31. A woman's work is never done.

32. Have not, want not.

33. All good things come to an end.

34. Too many cooks spoil the broth.

(continued)

PROVERBS

35. Home is where the heart is.

36. Never swap horses in the middle of the stream.

37. A watched pot never boils.

38. Beauty is in the eye of the beholder.

39. Better late than never.

40. Better safe than sorry.

41. Blood is thicker than water.

42. Boys will be boys.

43. Don't cast your pearls before swine.

44. Desperate times call for desperate measures.

45. Different strokes for different folks.

46. Don't burn your bridges before they're crossed.

47. Don't throw out the baby with the bathwater.

48. The early bird catches the worm.

49. Love is blind.

50. One good turn deserves another.

51. Don't put off until tomorrow what you should do today.

52. Honesty is the best policy.

53. Don't put the cart before the horse.

54. When it rains, it pours.

55. An ounce of prevention is worth a pound of cure.

56. Every cloud has a silver lining.

57. Familiarity breeds contempt.

58. History repeats itself.

59. Good fences make good neighbors.

60. His bark is worse than his bite.

61. The end justifies the means.

62. April showers bring May flowers.

63. Fool me once, shame on you. Fool me twice, shame on me.

64. Honey catches more flies than vinegar.

65. If a thing is worth doing, it's worth doing well.

66. The grass is always greener on the other side.

67. Kill two birds with one stone.

68. Let sleeping dogs lie.

69. Don't cut off your nose to spite your face.

70. One man's trash is another man's treasure.

71. It takes two to tango.

72. If you can't beat 'em, join 'em.

(continued)

73. Don't put all your eggs in one basket.

74. If anything can go wrong, it will.

75. Two heads are better than one.

76. There's more than one way to skin a cat.

77. Two's company. Three's a crowd.

78. If the shoe fits, wear it.

79. Truth is stranger than fiction.

80. Look before you leap.

81. Do as I say, not as I do.

82. Money makes the world go 'round.

83. No man is an island.

84. Laughter is the best medicine.

85. Out of sight, out of mind.

86. Don't rock the boat.

87. Practice makes perfect.

88. The pen is mightier than the sword.

89. Still waters run deep.

90. Talk is cheap.

91. You can't have your cake and eat it, too.

92. The best things in life are free.

93. Two wrongs don't make a right.

94. You can't teach an old dog new tricks.

95. Birds of a feather flock together.

96. You win some, you lose some.

97. Rules are made to be broken.

98. There's no such thing as a free lunch.

99. Misery loves company.

100. Time is money.

PROMPTS

1. You have just opened a gift from old Aunt Tilda. What is it and how do you react?

2. You are taking a test and suddenly you realize that the girl next to you is copying your answers. What will you do? What happens next?

3. You see someone pull the fire alarm as you are walking back to class from the bathroom. What do you do?

4. You have invented a new perfume with magical powers. Describe the perfume and show what it can do.

5. A bus driver has taken your class on a field trip. When she tries to turn the bus around, she runs the back wheel off the road, leaving the back of the bus hanging above the ditch. Everyone begins to scream. The bus is leaning to one side. What happens next?

6. A girl likes a boy who does not notice her. She goes to see someone who can give her a magical love potion to get the boy. How does it work? What happens next?

7. Describe perfection.

8. Invent a new reality television show. Describe the people who would compete and what the competition would be.

9. Create an advertisement for a new product. Make everyone want to buy it.

10. List ten new names for lipstick.

11. Give all the reasons students should wear uniforms to school.

12. Explain how to become the "teacher's pet."

13. You have received a hideous present from someone and you decide to put it up for auction on eBay. Write the ad so that someone might actually want to buy it.

14. Write a "slow news day" story. For instance, tell about how perfectly healthy people are parking in the handicapped spaces or how many people steal napkins from fast food places. Make the ordinary story sound extraordinary.

15. You are about to kill a roach, and the roach begins talking to you begging for his life. Now what happens?

16. Go on strike. Think of a mundane job you hate (like cleaning your room or answering questions at the end of a chapter) and write to the person in charge, telling why you are refusing to continue the task.

17. You have morphed into an animal. Describe your new life.

(continued)

18. Invent a new holiday. Convince everyone to celebrate with you.

19. You open a fortune cookie with a bizarre fortune. To your dismay, the fortune starts to come true...

20. The CIA is following you. You have just found a tracking device in your shoe. Why is this happening to you?

21. You are looking for the perfect outfit to wear to a party. Suddenly an article of clothing grabs you and says, "Take me home!"

22. Write a conversation between two people. Write what each person actually says, but also include what each person is *really* thinking.

23. Invent a new contest. Write the rules and decide what the prize will be.

24. Your friend is going to appear on *Dr. Phil.* What is your friend's problem and what do you think will happen on the show?

25. Write a list of things *not* to take on a picnic.

26. You are dreaming. When you try to wake up, you discover that the dream has become your reality...

27. You have been unjustly accused of doing something. What happened and what will you do?

28. You are babysitting and something weird happens...

29. Your mom makes you go into Goodwill with her. Inside you see the most popular person in the school. Now what happens?

30. You have just drunk a liquid that makes you invisible. Now what will you do?

31. You have been called to the office of the assistant principal. Tell us the conversation that takes place in the office.

32. Your best friend (or mom or dad) has just morphed into a creature. What happened and what happens next?

33. Describe a world in which there is no color...

34. You have just won a million dollars. What will you do with the money?

35. Imagine that you have been adopted. You are about to meet one of your biological parents for the first time. What is the meeting like? What do you say?

36. Your girlfriend (or boyfriend) is under lots of stress. She doesn't have time to complete a huge assignment for school. She begs you to do it for her. What do you do?

37. Imagine that you *have* to go back in time to live. Once you choose the place, you cannot return to the present. Where will you go and why?

38. You have learned to fly. You try to tell some trusted friends, but no one believes you. What will you do with your new ability?

(continued)

PROMPTS

39. You are visiting a museum with your class. A person in a painting you are looking at comes to life. What happens next?

40. You have just said to your friend, "It looks like it's going to rain cats and dogs." Suddenly cats and dogs begin to fall from the sky! Now what happens?

41. You have discovered that you have the ability to control or stop time. What will you do with your new ability?

42. Tell how *not* to do something—how *not* to get your parents to let you go somewhere, how *not* to get a date, how *not* to cut your hair, etc.

43. Think of a moral choice someone has to make, but the right choice is not crystal clear. Describe the situation and the choice you would make.

44. List five things that frustrate you. Then write about how you could "fix" one of them.

45. Imagine that the room is suddenly upside down. You have to walk on the ceiling and the floor becomes the new ceiling. How did this happen? What happens next?

46. What if you suddenly gained forty pounds? How would your life change?

47. You are talking to people, but no one can hear you.

48. Suddenly you have hypersensitive hearing and can hear things others can't. Describe something you overhear and what happens next.

49. You are in a foreign country with a friend. You get very lost. You do not speak the language. How do you get help?

50. You have a magic flashlight. When you shine it on someone's heart, you can see the person's most protected secrets. What secrets are revealed to you? Leave out names.

51. Why have you just robbed a bank? What were you thinking?

52. No one around you has any hair. But you do. What happened?

53. What are the root causes of prejudices? What can be done to eliminate them?

54. What makes a person a hero? Who are the heroes in your life?

55. List ten new color names.

56. Write five new bumper stickers.

57. Your life is a videotape. You get to go back and redo a part of the video. What scene do you choose to re-tape?

58. Think of something about yourself that you really like. How can you spread this characteristic to others?

59. Describe your favorite class in school, ever. Why did (or do) you like it?

(continued)

60. Describe your favorite teacher, ever. What qualities make that teacher effective?

61. Write a top ten list for something: the top ten reasons you should skip to the next grade, the top ten indications that the party was a bad idea, the top ten hints that someone doesn't like you, etc.

62. Describe your least favorite teacher in school. (Leave out any mention of the name.) What did this person do to earn your dislike?

63. What can you tell from a person's hands?

64. If you could live anywhere in the world, where would you live and why?

65. What would happen if all the computers in the world stopped working?

66. What lasting impact has 9/11 had on the lives of those in the United States?

67. You are attending a funeral of a relative and the person suddenly sits up and starts talking...

68. Think about something bad that happened to you but that actually had a positive impact on your life. Write about it.

69. Describe a romantic date that costs very little money.

70. You wake up to find out you can only see in black and white. What happened and what will you do?

71. List ways you can tell someone is "just not that into you."

72. What is the perfect pet? Explain.

73. Imagine that you are a brand new teacher. You have just been hired to teach the "class from hell." Describe your first day.

74. You discover bomb-making materials in your neighbor's garage. What do you do?

75. Invent a new cell phone ring and persuade others to use it.

76. If a "white lie" is a lie told to spare a person's feelings or to protect someone, what would a "black lie" be? Give some examples.

77. Describe a person who is obsessive-compulsive.

78. What would you definitely do if money were no object? Why?

79. Imagine that you have become a celebrity. Describe a typical day.

80. A young parent is shopping in the mall with a baby. Someone snatches the child. Now what happens?

81. Fast-forward your life by ten years. What is your life like now?

82. You are on the *Jerry Springer Show* with four other people? How did you get there? What happens?

(continued)

83. One of your friends smells really bad. You don't want to hurt his feelings, but you don't want to be around him. What do you do?

84. You meet a mystery guy/girl online. You both decide to meet at a restaurant. When you arrive, you discover that the mystery person is someone you know. Now what do you do?

85. You are watching your friend's pet while he is on vacation. The pet dies because of something that you did (or didn't do). How do you take care of this problem?

86. Your best friend just regifted you with the same present you gave him last year. Do you say anything or just accept the gift?

87. You wake up with your mouth sewn shut and you're wearing a straight jacket. The last thing you remember is your mother yelling at you...

88. You receive a package at the front door of your home. When you pick it up, you hear a ticking noise...

89. You see the picture of your best friend on a milk carton saying he/she's lost. Now what?

90. You have been shrunk and put into a water bottle. How did you get there? What will you do?

91. You get bored on a blind date. How do you tell your date you want to go home?

92. You are the owner of a thrift shop. An old man in his late eighties comes in and you see him shoplifting. Do you stop him or let him go? Why or why not?

93. Does everyone deserve a second chance? Justify your answer.

94. We all put up walls to protect ourselves from others. What are some of the walls you have around yourself or that you see around others? (Use with Robert Frost's "Mending Wall.")

95. Which of your senses could you most easily live without? Justify your choice. (Use with *The Miracle Worker*.)

96. What if animals took over the world? Which animals would be in charge? Which animals would be followers? How would people fit in? (Use with *Animal Farm*.)

97. Think of a place from childhood like a tree house, a favorite store, your grandmother's house, etc. Now go back and revisit it in your mind. How does it look now? How has it changed? How does it make you feel? (Use with *A Separate Peace*.)

98. Robert Frost describes how "Two roads diverged in a yellow wood." Think of a time in your life when you had to make a decision to go one way or another. Which way did you go? How did you decide? Did you make the right decision?

(continued)

99. Write a one-page poem that captures the essence of *you*. (Use with the Langston Hughes' poem "Theme for English B.")

100. Victor Hugo describes the lives of miserable people in *Les Miserables*. Who are our "miserable ones" in today's society? Whose fault is it that they are miserable? Can they be helped? How?

101. The Scarlet Pimpernel dresses up in disguises to save people in *The Scarlet Pimpernel*. Invent your own character who disguises himself to help others.

102. In *To Kill a Mockingbird*, Scout and Jem find many objects that represent their childhood, hidden in a hollow tree. What objects would represent your childhood? Explain.

103. Masks enable us to face the world and adopt new identities. What mask do you wear? How does it change you? What hides behind your mask? (Use with *Phantom of the Opera.*)

104. You have just met the love of your life. It was love at first sight. Describe the event in detail. (Use with *Romeo and Juliet.*)

105. Thoreau said he went to the woods for two years to "live life deliberately." How would you change your life to live it deliberately? (Use with *Walden.*)

106. Winston Smith is taken to Room 101 in the book *1984*. There he is confronted with his greatest fear. What would be your greatest fear in Room 101?

107. You have just inherited a great sum of money from an anonymous source. Who do you think gave it to you? Why? (Use with *Great Expectations.*)

108. Which emotion is more destructive— guilt or jealousy? Explain. (Use with *A Separate Peace.*)

APPENDIX

Student Examples

TABLOID STORY, PAGE 17

Original Headline: "Patient Begs Doctor to Cut off His Leg."
Story:

LEG

Clair Shidler

"Dr. Lewis's office. How may I help you?" answered a cheerful voice.

"I need to make an appointment," a painful voice responded.

"Okay then, sir, I just need you...," Tom didn't hear anything else the nurse said except when he should come in. He was about to fulfill his dream. He hung up the phone and turned to his friends.

"I did it. I made the appointment." His friends stared at him with disgust. Tom had been hanging around this place for about three years now, and his "friends" still stared at him the same way. He knew he didn't really fit in. He picked up his crutches and hobbled out of the room.

When he got home, he took out his special box. Here he kept his plans for his surgery "before" pictures of him and "after" pictures of people he would look like after his surgery. He decided to take the box to his appointment on Wednesday. All his life he had dreamed about this day and the way he would feel once the surgery was done.

Early Wednesday morning Tom woke up and started to get ready. He took a shower, carefully balancing himself on one leg, and cooked breakfast the same way. Tom then got his crutches and wobbled to his car. It was 9:00 a.m. and he didn't have to be there until 10:00 a.m., but he was so excited that he decided to get there an hour early. He walked into the office and slowly made his way to the window to sign in.

"Good morning, sir. Please have a seat and the doctor will see you soon." Tom took his seat and opened a magazine. He read an article for about thirty minutes and then he heard his name.

"Right here!" Tom reached for his crutches and hobbled into the examination room to wait for the doctor. The nurse questioned him about his past medical history, medicines he was taking, and what the doctor could do for him today.

"I would feel more comfortable talking to the doctor about what I am here for," he told the nurse.

"I understand, sir. He will be here in a few minutes." The nurse closed the door on her way out. Tom sat in the padded chair and twiddled his thumbs nervously.

"Tom Davis? I'm Doctor Lewis. What can I do for you today?"

"Well, Doc, I need you to cut this leg off." Tom said it so fast the doctor barely understood him. For a few minutes the doctor just stared at him in disbelief.

"Why do you need me to do that?" the doctor questioned.

"I am ugly with four limbs. I am an ugly duckling, but with three limbs I will be beautiful. I will be perfect!"

STUDENT EXAMPLES

"Do you have any medical problems with the leg?"

"Yes, it won't do what I want it to do," Tom answered.

"Tom, what do you want your leg to do exactly?"

" I want it to fall off," he replied bluntly.

"Have you seen another kind of doctor about this obsession?"

"Yes, and she told me the only way I will be better is to have it cut off."

"I have good news for you then; I have done this operation before and I will do it for you, too. I want you to understand that the surgery is very painful," the doctor said. Tom started crying and said he understood.

"Mr. Davis, do you hang around amputees?"

"Yes, sir, I do and to tell you the truth, I don't think they like me all that much."

"You're going to have to stop doing that once the operation has been done," Dr. Lewis told him harshly. For the next hour they discussed the way the operation would be done, the date, and the cost. Tom left feeling like a new person. He went home and pondered what the doctor had told him. It comforted him to know that the doctor had done this before.

During the middle of the night Tom sat straight up in his bed. It hit him that the doctor only had one leg. He reached for the phone and called Dr. Lewis at home.

"Hello," a groggy voice answered.

"This is Tom. Did you cut off your own leg?"

"Now, Tom, that is my personal business, but, yes, I did." Tom was so shocked he hung up the phone and lay back down. He thought how weird that was. He began to think about his own leg and what would be done with it after it was cut off. It was part of him.

He stood up, and for the first time in four years, he walked on two legs to the bathroom. Tom turned on the light and gazed in the full-length mirror. He was twenty-five and had never even had a date. That was when he realized that it wasn't his leg that made him ugly; it was his whole outlook on life.

The next day Tom made an appointment with a psychiatrist and started his journey to change his life.

ELEVATOR STORY, PAGE 19

Elevator stories need not take place in an elevator, although this one does.

ELEVATOR STORY
Amanda Rivers

Today is the first day of the creative writing class. Nobody knows anybody yet, except the twin boys on the left. But here they all are, standing in this elevator together, waiting to get to floor fourteen.

It's quiet. The students are anxious. Sure, they've had writing classes before. But this is the class taught by renowned author, academy-award winner, and baby-saver, Mrs. Karla T.B. Hardaway. The "T.B." stands for "Totally Beast." And yes—that is what her parents named her. It's even written on her birth certificate. So it must be true...and it is. After all, this lady has written twenty-two best-selling novels, starred in eighteen films, won eighteen Academy Awards, and saved nine whole babies. Totally Beast.

The students fidget here and there as the elevator rises. They watch the floor dial move slowly past ten, to eleven, to twelve, and finally...

But wait! The elevator comes to a complete stop! The floor dial vibrates uncertainly between the numbers twelve and fourteen, then stays there, hovering.

The doors do not open. No sound is made. For a brief moment, the students stare at each other. And then, a resounding "Oh, no!" is heard. Everyone looks to see where it came from. Their eyes rest on two boys—twins, with the same longish black hair and denim blue eyes, standing against the mirrored left wall.

"It's okay," a girl with a blonde ponytail says in a nice, clear voice. "Just a minute and it'll be running again. This probably happens all the time here."

A murmur of uncertain agreement echoes from the other students.

"Yah, it happened the other day, and it was just, like two minutes."

"You'd think they'd have fixed this by now."

"Glad I'm not claustrophobic..." There's some nervous laughter.

"But it's not okay."

Once again, their eyes fall on the twin boys.

"Don't you get it?" one of the twins asks loudly.

"This is an elevator story!" the other twin finishes.

A confused pause, and then voices rise up in response.

"You're dumb."

"What the straw, kid? It'll be a second, and the elevator will be working again."

"Yah! Stop trying to freak people out. It's not even working."

"Why would you even say that?"

"Besides, there's, like, no one here that could cause conflict. Nobody here's mentally ill. There are no crazed killers, and no one's having a medical emergency." The girl with the blonde ponytail is watching the twin boys now. She seems amused.

"Oh, really? No crazed killers?" the twins continue, taking turns.

"What about the guy in the back corner? Dark green shirt? Weed Whacker?"

The students turn to look.

"Uh, I'm Steve...I'm not a serial killer," an awkward boy in his late teens answers uncomfortably, all eyes on him.

A pause. Now another rise of voices.

"Who brings a Weed Whacker onto an elevator?" The blonde's ponytail flies back and forth.

"It's been, like two minutes...When's it going to start up again?" a redheaded boy wails.

"I wanna see Mrs. Hardaway !!! I'm her number one fan!!!" Weed Whacker Steve yells.

"Shut up!"

"Steve eats babies!!!" one of the twins sings out.

"I do not!!"

"I think we're really stuck, guys..." This statement from a boy in the front silences the rest quickly. The crowd gives him their attention. He has a messy haircut and is wearing an AC/DC T-shirt. His expression is sour.

"How long now?" someone calls.

"Like five minutes."

"Isn't there one of those red phone things?" someone else offers.

"No," AC/DC T-shirt answers with a big sigh. "Guess we're stuck here for a while."

The twins look at each other, grinning. "Elevator story!!!"

"Quiet, you two." The blonde is suddenly serious. "Look, nobody panic. It won't be very long before they realize this elevator isn't working—it's the middle of the day! They'll send a handyman up here to solve the problem in no time."

Ten minutes pass...

"Her, for example..." one of the twins whispers to the blonde. He motions to a mousy looking girl with stringy black hair and thick, horn-rimmed glasses, engulfed in a giant brown sweater. She crouches against the right wall; stares down at the red carpeting. Clicks her fingernails. Click, click, click, click, click, click.

"Would you cut it out?" the redheaded boy next to her exclaims, throwing her a look.

The girl doesn't look up, but stops. Now she taps the toes of her shoes against the carpet instead, like trading one nervous tick for another.

"Totally unstable," the other twin continues in a whisper.

There is a comfortable buzz of chatter now, the students working out their nerves through conversation.

"Or that one!" one of the twins laughs, nodding towards the AC/DC T-shirt boy who is blaring rock music through his headphones. "Look at his face! Ha! I don't think he's all there!"

The AC/DC T-shirt boy with the headphones has a deadpan expression, vacant blue eyes, and his mouth hangs open slightly. His head bobs out of rhythm to the music.

The blonde laughs and glances around the space, looking for her own person to analyze. "What about her? She's all flushed. Looks like she's about to..."

The quiet, dark-haired girl who has been silent so far suddenly collapses into a pile on the floor on top of the redheaded boy and two girls near him. Thud, thud, thud, thud.

Three minutes pass...Eleven bodies lie in various poses all over the floor. The AC/DC T-shirt boy stands alone, a stun gun in his hand. He pushes a button.

A whirring noise. The elevator starts back up. It reaches the fourteenth floor. The boy steps out and walks into the classroom.

"Sorry I'm late, Mrs. Hardaway. I had to finish my elevator story."

"I don't care! Have a seat!"

The AC/DC T-shirt boy walks to the back of the crowded room and takes a seat in the last empty desk.

MEMOIRS, PAGE 20

JIMMIE BONES
Jameka Barber

"Mooke, go get in the tub before I tell Grandma!" I taunted my younger cousin.

"Okay, okay, Meka, I going. Don't tell!" she shrieked running into the bathroom and jumping into the tub. I giggled but stopped when my grandma yelled up the stairs.

"What in the world are y'all doing up there? Don't make me come up these steps!"

I had to put my hand over my mouth to keep from laughing. Walking into the bathroom to make sure Mooke was washing herself right, I began thinking about last night when my daddy had called. I had been sitting on the edge of the bed watching television in my grandparents' room when the phone rang.

"Jimmie, give me the phone," my grandma sleepily asked my granddad.

"Okay, honey, here." He handed her the phone and flopped back on his side to go back to sleep.

"Hey, baby, Mama been missing you and your chi...hold on, hold on, slow down and say it again," she said gently into the phone.

I knew who was on the phone. It was my daddy. I could tell something was wrong because of the look on my grandma's face, worried. Being a typical eleven-year-old, I began whining and begging to talk to my father. I knew I wasn't supposed to bother her while she was on the phone but this had to be an exception. I mean, it was my daddy.

"Grams, please, please, please, can I talk to my daddy?" My request hung in the air unnoticed, so I tried a different tactic.

"Grams, can you tell my daddy that I love him?" This time she looked at me but didn't relay my message. Instead she hung up the phone.

"Your daddy was busy and couldn't talk," she told me gently. I knew that wasn't the truth because she told my granddad that my dad had an argument with my stepmom earlier that day. My stepmom hadn't come home and my dad was worried because he didn't know where she was.

STUDENT EXAMPLES

As I got Mooke out of the tub and dried her off, I mused about what my dad and stepmother could have been arguing about. The sound of something falling on the floor followed by my grandma's yell had me running down the stairs to see if she was okay.

At the foot of the steps was a wireless phone. I picked it up and quickly replaced the receiver.

"Grandma!" I yelled, rushing into the living room thinking she had burned herself. She was crumpled on the floor crying so hard her shoulders were rocking.

I didn't know what to think or what to do. I just dropped to my knees next to her and wrapped my arms around her and began rocking. I told her everything was okay; everything would be fine. I didn't know what else to say.

She tried to tell me something, but the words were lost in her sobs. After a couple of shaky deep breaths, she finally told me what was wrong.

I didn't think I heard her clearly. It almost sounded like she said someone had died. There is no way I heard her clearly. No one dies in my family. She took both of my hands and said in a crystal clear voice, "Baby...your daddy is gone."

I just stared at her not understanding what she meant by gone. Gone? Gone how? She saw that I wasn't understanding or wasn't letting myself understand, so she rephrased her statement. "Danielle, baby, your daddy is dead."

Now I knew I hadn't heard her right! Was this some kind of sick joke? How could he be dead? She had just talked to him last night! Somewhere deep in my heart I knew it was true. It felt like someone used a dull knife to cut my heart out and stuffed the severed part into my lungs. I couldn't breathe, talk, or have a coherent thought. All I could do was bury my face in her arms and cry.

"Awe, baby, it's okay. Grand-Mamma's here. I know it hurts. Just let it out," she murmured into my hair.

"I don't understand! How can he be dead? You just talked to him last night!" I shouted as she rocked me. The moment the question left my lips, I knew I couldn't handle the answer.

"They said it was suicide. Maria came home and found him lying on the bed; he died in the ambulance on the way to the hospital." She whispered the words so low that I could barely hear her. All I could do was cry. My emotions were so strong and raw in my chest. My mind could only make a single coherent thought. My daddy was dead and I didn't get the chance to say good-bye.

This story is dedicated to my father Jimmie Barber (also known as Jimmie Bones).

GRAVEYARD SCAVENGER HUNT, PAGE 21
COMING HOME

Ellen Sweeney

Rachel sat at her desk typing a report for Doctor Neville. Her eyes had more bags under them; the stress from caring for two children alone was taking its toll on her once youthful appearance. She sighed as the phone rang.

"Hello, is Mrs. Odell in?" A rough male voice came through the phone.

"This is she. How may I help you, sir?" Rachel looked at the clock. Three minutes until she got off.

"This is Colonel Sam Buckner. I was wondering if you could come to the counseling center tonight? We are having a briefing session. My wife and Tina Cossner will be on hand to watch the children." He sounded very distracted.

"Sure, I'd love to come. What time?" The thought of being around other army wives sent a jolt of electricity through her.

"Seven, in room 312. I'll see you tonight."

Rachel hung up the phone. She decided to grab some dinner on the road and feed the kids quickly. She hadn't been to an army wife meeting since her husband Hunter left for Vietnam. He had been gone nearly a year. Only four more months and he would be home. The thought of Hunter being back home with her and the kids was enough to make her smile and laugh out into the empty waiting room.

At room 312 Rachel opened the door to see Chaplin Morris and Colonel Buckner sitting in front of five other women. She knew them as the wives of Hunter's regiment. Chaplin Morris smiled at her and motioned to the couch.

"Please, come and sit down, Rachel. We all need to speak." Chaplin Morris always had a soft voice. He was an older man, a little hunched with hair that was slightly balding.

Rachel took a seat by Becky, a woman she had become close friends with in Hunter's absence. Colonel Buckner looked down at the pile of folders in his lap with a sigh and then back up to the faces of the women in front of him.

"Ladies, this past weekend we received news that your husbands were abducted. We aren't sure where they are or what has happened to them. We are spending all the time and energy we can on finding them and getting them back safe and sound. Please understand that this is now the most important item on our agenda. We hope that Chaplin Morris can help you through this time. We offer free counseling and support for you and your family. You are the first that we have called; we do hope that your husbands will be found safe and sound."

Rachel sat there dumbfounded. What? Why? No, not her Hunter! And not Becky's Mason! She looked to the floor, not sure of how to react. Worst of all, how would she tell her children? How dare they take her husband away! Who could do such a thing? And then Rachel fainted into the black chaos of the floor.

Twenty years later...

An aged Rachel sat alone at the kitchen table reading the newspaper when the phone rang.

"Mrs. Odell, this is Sergeant Stripes. We have good news. We found your husband. His remains were in a cave. He is coming home."

Three weeks later Rachel was sitting in the back of a limo following a hearse containing Hunter's casket. All the military fuss couldn't hide the fact that he was really gone. She had

STUDENT EXAMPLES

kept some vague hope alive that he would one day saunter through the door and smile at her. She whispered to him all the things he had missed; their children growing up and having children, herself aging.

"Oh Hunter, welcome home. I truly missed you," Rachel whispered as they pulled up to his graveside. The new tombstone read:

Hunter Scott Odell
Born September 15, 1950
Missing in Action March 13, 1978
Vietnam Veteran
Body interred August 12, 1998

At Rest Lies an American Soldier
And Defender of the Constitution.
Don't cry for me...I've met my destiny and
finally found solace in the soil that covers me.

Survived by his loving wife Rachel
and children Parker and Claire

METAPHORS, PAGE 59

I AM

Anna Atkinson

I am the vase with no flowers
Sitting awkwardly on the bookshelf.
I am the crack in the tile
That sits uniformly with the others.
I am a crumpled piece of paper
Cradling secrets inside.
I am a picture on the wall.
No—
I am the space behind the picture.
I am the dust on the windowpane
Crying out for attention.
I am everything you don't see.

FRUIT SALAD

Lindsay Oar

I'll be the grapes
You be the strawberries
We'll find a bowl
Maybe a spoon
The sugar will be our love
And together...
We'll be the fruit salad
That we'll eat at noon.

I'D HAVE THE BULLET, I SAY
Justin Runyon

Which of these would I eat, you ask?
Bullet, dagger, arsenic?
I'd order a bullet at least,
I say.
I love the texture and culinary history behind it.
All the men who have dined with the bullet—
King, Kennedy, Lincoln—
All had a bullet for their last meal.

QUILT
Ann Barr

I rescue an old quilt
With frayed, yellow edges
From a flea market vendor
For five dollars.

I imagine the maker threading a needle by lamplight.
She searches through hoarded scraps
To create a work of art.
Each scrap evokes memories
Of events and people.

I vow to remember her.
I pray to inherit her patience
Along with her quilt.
I want my life to become a
Treasure of hoarded memories
Woven into life's fabric and
Passed on to future generations.

ABOUT THE AUTHOR

Karla Hardaway taught English, speech, debate, and creative writing in Louisiana for thirty-four years and was very active in training new teachers and implementing new teaching methods. She has presented countless teaching workshops and also taught in Louisiana's STAR (Students Teaching and Reaching) program. She is the mother of four children and currently lives in Shreveport, Louisiana, with her husband Steven.

Find more great books from Cottonwood Press, Inc., at
www.cottonwoodpress.com.

COTTONWOODPRESS INC.